Education in England and Wales

H. C. Dent

LINNET BOOKS

Photography by Henry Grant, AIIP

Library of Congress Cataloging in Publication Data

Dent, Harold Collett, 1894–
  Education in England and Wales.

  First-5th ed. published under title: The educational system of England and
Wales.
Including bibliographical and index.
  1. Education—England—History. 2. Education—Wales—History.
3. Comparative education. I. Title.
LA631.D385 1977 370'.942 77-12936
ISBN 0–208–01742–9

Printed and bound in Great Britain.

Contents

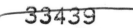

Preface

What I attempt to do in this book is to give a concise yet comprehensive description of the organization and conduct of education in England and Wales, together with a brief outline of its history.

I bring the story down to the end of 1976. As so many changes are taking place, very rapidly, by the time the book is published some items in it will already be outdated. I urge readers to keep abreast with events by study of the educational press.

I am indebted, as always, to many friends for help. I would like on this occasion to thank particularly Mr Ralph Brooke, headmaster of the Joseph Whitaker Comprehensive School, Rainworth, Nottinghamshire. I am grateful once again to Mr Stanley Foster of Hodder and Stoughton Educational and his colleagues for their friendly and efficient services.

For the contents of the book I am, of course, solely responsible.

Whatlington, East Sussex, 12 March 1977　　　　　　　　　　　　　H C Dent

CHAPTER 1 | # Genealogical Tree

The story of organized education in England and Wales begins with the bringing of Christianity to Kent in A.D. 597. No direct evidence exists to support this statement, but there can be little doubt that when St Augustine established his cathedral church at Canterbury he included among its functions the teaching of converts and the training of native ministers of the Church. Such was the invariable practice of the Christian missionaries of those days; to them, religion and education were inseparable, and both equally the business of the Church.

As Christianity spread across England similar 'schools' were set up in other cathedrals, in collegiate churches, and in monasteries. In the earliest days these schools had neither buildings nor staff of their own; they were merely assemblies of pupils – of all ages – taught by the bishop himself or one of his priestly colleagues, in some convenient part of the church. But gradually the distinction was drawn (as it had long been in other parts of the Roman Empire) between 'grammar', or general education, and the simpler and more directly vocational training which was all that was required by novices aspiring to be members of church choirs and to assist as acolytes the priests in the performance of the church services. Increasingly, 'Grammar' and 'Song' schools tended to draw apart.

'Grammar', which then meant the Latin language and literature, was the first of the Seven Liberal Arts[1] of medieval Christian scholarship; and not merely the first, but "the foundation, gate and source of all the other liberal arts, without which such arts cannot be known, nor can anyone arrive at practising them".[2] Latin was the universal language of religion, law and government throughout Christendom, and therefore essential not only to scholars but also to all aiming at a career in the service of Church or State. It is not surprising that from the start the Grammar school enjoyed a higher status, and was staffed by better paid teachers, than the Song school.

As time went on it became not infrequent for the English Grammar school to demand that its pupils should on entry be literate in their native language. To meet this demand there developed the Reading and Writing school, sometimes as a preparatory department to a Grammar or Song school, sometimes as a separate establishment.

During the later Middle Ages the Song school tended to fade out of existence altogether or to merge with the Reading and Writing school in what was called the 'Pettie' (i.e. *petite*, for little children) school, the medieval equivalent of the modern Elementary, or Primary, school. The Grammar school has had a continuous history right down to the present day. Several existing schools, such as, for example, the King's School, Canterbury, St Peter's, York, Beverley Grammar School, St Albans, Sherborne, and Warwick, can claim, if not an uninterrupted life, at least direct descent from schools founded long before the Norman Conquest.

Before the rise of the universities the English Grammar school often undertook the teaching of rhetoric, and sometimes dialectic, as well as grammar, and in exceptional cases – as under Alcuin at York in the eighth century – grew to be university and theological college as well as school, with a curriculum covering almost the entire range of medieval learning. With the emergence of Oxford during the second half of the twelfth century and of Cambridge in the early years of the thirteenth its scope was increasingly confined to the teaching of grammar, and one of its most important functions became that of preparing able pupils for entry into the University. This function the Grammar school has ever since retained.

From the fourteenth century onwards many Grammar schools were founded with this purpose expressly in mind, being either attached to or linked by scholarships with Colleges at Oxford or Cambridge. An example of great historical importance was 'Seint Marie College at Wynchester', founded by William of Wykeham, Bishop of Winchester, in 1382. This foundation made a crucial departure from previous practice. All previous schools – or so it is claimed – had been ancillary to various other establishments: they had been parts of cathedrals, collegiate churches, monasteries, chantries, hospitals, or university colleges. But Winchester College, though a twin foundation with Wykeham's 'Seint Marie College of Wynchester in Oxenford' (New College, Oxford), and designed to supply this with scholars, was nevertheless created for the sole purpose of providing a school. "Thus for the first time," wrote A. F. Leach, "a school was established as a sovereign and independent corporation, existing by and for itself, self-centred and self-governed."[3] Other benefactors followed Wykeham's example; notable among them was Henry VI, who when he founded Eton College in 1440 modelled its statutes closely upon those of Winchester.

Some historians have seen in the terms of the foundation deed of Winchester College the origins of the English 'Public' school. Not so much, perhaps, because of the independence accorded to the College, important though this was, as because of three other conditions. Pupils were to be accepted from anywhere in England (though certain counties had priority), the College was to be largely a boarding-school, and it was to include among its boarders, in addition to the seventy 'poor and indigent' scholars (*pauperes et indigentes*)[4] for whom free places were provided, up to ten 'sons of noble and influential persons' who would pay fees for their tuition and their keep.

How 'noble and influential' Wykeham hoped the parents of his fee-paying boarders would be one cannot say; but he does not appear to have been successful in attracting those of highest rank. This was simply because it was not the habit of the English aristocracy in the Middle Ages – or for long afterwards –

to send their sons to school. They provided for them, in their own homes and those of their peers, an exclusive, and totally different, form of education, aimed at the attainment of skill in the arts of war and the etiquette of chivalry.

The Grammar school was in medieval England (there were few schools in Wales) the avenue of opportunity for the able sons of parents of relatively modest means – the lesser gentry, yeoman farmers, merchants and craftsmen, and, occasionally, villeins or serfs. It led to careers in Church and State and in the learned and clerical professions. Neither poverty nor lowly status in society was an absolute bar to entry; almost all Grammar schools had, like Winchester and Eton, free places for 'poor and indigent' pupils, and any boy whose ability excited the interest of the parish priest or the local squire could be awarded one of these; and, later, make his way to the University by winning one of the scholarships which many schools had to offer.

Not all such parents sent their sons to Grammar school and University. For those who thought more in terms of worldly wealth there was, from the twelfth century onwards, the highly organized system of apprenticeship run by the powerful craft and merchant guilds, whereby a boy was bound by indentures to a master-craftsman, who took him into his home for an agreed number of years and taught him his trade, thus enabling him in his turn to become a master-craftsman or merchant. Many of the smaller gentry chose this medieval equivalent of technical education for their younger sons, to whom – the law of primogeniture being absolute – they would have no goods to leave.

Modern research has shown that elementary education[5] was far more widely prevalent in medieval England than was formerly believed. Much of it was given by parish priests, who from an early date were constantly being reminded by their bishops that it was their duty to undertake it. Much was given in the numerous chantries founded during the later Middle Ages. The first duty of a chantry priest was to say Masses for the souls of the founder and such other persons as were specified in the foundation deed. But as this was rarely a full-time occupation, the priest was frequently instructed also to 'kepe a grammar skole' or to teach the children of the district 'to rede and sing'. By the time of the Reformation there were over 2,000 chantries in England. How many undertook teaching is unknown; perhaps in most cases only when the priest was sufficiently interested to take the initiative. According to the Chantry Certificates of Edward VI the majority of the fully organized chantry schools were Grammar schools, but there was also an appreciable number of 'pettie' schools. In the 'pettie' school girls as well as boys were often to be found. But girls were rarely, if ever, admitted into the Grammar school, nor was any comparable type of school provided for them, though a few received some sort of secondary education in nunneries. Girls' education, beyond the rudiments, was normally undertaken in the home, and consisted of training in domestic duties.

For close on a thousand years, from the coming of St Augustine to the Reformation, the Church controlled absolutely, and was almost exclusively the provider of, all organized education, other than the training of apprentices and aristocrats, from the group of village children taught by the parish or chantry priest to the societies of scholars in the Colleges of Oxford and Cambridge. Every teacher had to be licensed by the bishop, who also – in the early days personally, and later through his deputies the chancellor and the precentor – appointed all Grammar and Song school headmasters. With but rare exceptions all teachers were clerks in the orders of the Church. The Church claimed a monopoly in education, and though this was from the twelfth century onwards occasionally disputed, in practice it was most effectively maintained.

The contribution made by the laity became substantial as a result of the English Reformation. It used to be believed that the dissolution of the monasteries and the expropriation of the chantries by Henry VIII and Edward VI had a disastrous effect upon English education. Recent research[6] has shown this opinion to be incorrect. The chantries and monasteries were at the time of their closure doing far less educational work than was previously estimated. The Commissioners who investigated the affairs of the chantries "took the most elaborate pains to protect existing schools".[7] And – infinitely more important in the long run – the closures moved a host of benefactors, chiefly rich merchants (especially London merchants) and landed gentry, but including also royalty, nobility, clergy, municipalities, and guilds, to re-establish and re-endow grammar schools that would otherwise have ceased to exist, and to found many new schools as well. At these schools they often endowed scholarships to the universities, or alternatively established at the colleges which were growing up at Oxford and Cambridge 'closed' scholarships, available only to boys (girls were still not considered to need academic learning) attending a specified school or resident in a particular locality.

This great movement, which resulted in the foundation, or re-foundation, of hundreds of Grammar schools, almost all with free places for necessitous pupils, began to gather momentum during the earlier decades of the sixteenth century, expanded suddenly after the Reformation, and reached a high peak between 1611 and 1630. Professor W. K. Jordan has estimated that by 1660 there was a grammar school for each 4,400 of the population[8] – a proportion not to be reached again before the twentieth century.

During the Cromwellian interlude it looked for a moment as though a State system was on the way. Educational reform was in the air, and proposals were advanced for establishing a national system of elementary education. These, alas, came to nothing, except in Wales, where, under an Act for the Better Propagation of the Gospel, passed in 1650, nearly sixty free schools were established and maintained out of public funds. But they lasted only until the Restoration; and more than two centuries were to elapse before they had any successors.

During the eighteenth century Grammar school and University education fell to a very low ebb. Schools and Colleges alike resisted all attempts to induce them to move with the times, and clung persistently to outdated curricula and methods. Consequently, they became less and less capable of performing useful service to society, which naturally turned elsewhere for aid in meeting its educational needs. By the end of the century many Grammar schools had been closed and many more had but a handful of pupils; and the Universities of Oxford and Cambridge had largely become exclusive clubs for slothful dons who did not teach and wealthy young aristocrats who did not even pretend to study.

This unhappy situation was part cause and part effect of the fact that during this century both class and denominational distinctions hardened. England became riven into Disraeli's 'Two Nations', with on the one side of the great divide the tiny *élite* of the rich and privileged, and on the other the vast mass of the 'lower orders', the 'labouring poor', to which was added, towards the end of the century, the rising class of manufacturers and merchants that was being born out of the fast-developing Industrial Revolution. The line of denominational cleavage, while not identical, was not greatly different; the *élite*, almost to a man, adhered to the Established Church, while the strength of Nonconformity – immensely reinforced by John Wesley's half-century of fervent evangelism – lay with the lower orders and, most importantly, the new middle class that industry was throwing up.

The members of this class rejected with contempt the arid and unrealistic curricula of the Grammar schools and Universities (from the latter many of them were in any case excluded by their religious affiliations), and began to patronize private schools offering more modern – and more efficient – education for their children, and 'Dissenting Academies', which provided courses of study of University calibre, and were not reserved, as were Oxford and Cambridge, for members of the Established Church. At much the same time the *élite* began to send its sons to a small group of expensive boarding-schools – Eton, Harrow and Winchester were among them – which were coming to be known as the 'great', or 'public', schools. For the children of the lower orders no education beyond the merest rudiments of literacy was considered either necessary or appropriate. Much public opinion, indeed, among both the *élite* and the industrialists would have denied them even this meagre modicum of instruction, believing that any education at all would render them dissatisfied with their lowly lot, and thus cause them to become a menace to the stability of society.

Yet it was during this period of rigid social stratification and denominational discrimination that the foundations were laid for today's statutory system of public education. One good which resulted from the existence of an immensely wealthy *élite* alongside a poverty-stricken proletariat was the realization by the former (thanks largely to the teaching of their Church) that their possession of great riches imposed upon them a moral obligation to contribute in charity to the well-being of the latter; and not only to their material but also, and even more importantly, to their spiritual well-being. The first step towards this was to enable the poor to understand 'the principles of the Christian religion'; and that meant teaching the poor to read.

Towards the close of the seventeenth century many societies sprang up to further this end. In 1698 a decision that was to prove of very great historical importance was taken when a newly-formed Society for Promoting Christian Knowledge (SPCK) resolved, at its first meeting, 'to further and promote that good design of erecting Catechetical schools in each parish in and about London.' The design prospered; the Society, which worked by prompting parishes to provide their own schools, was able very shortly to extend the range of its activities beyond London, and within a quarter of a century had established schools in many parts of Britain. A remarkable offshoot of its enterprise was the creation in Wales by one of its local correspondents, the Reverend Griffith Jones, of a vast system of 'Circulating' schools, manned by peripatetic teachers, in which between about 1730 and 1780 many thousands of children and adults learned to read.

During the second half of the eighteenth century the founding of weekday schools languished. The Industrial Revolution was sweeping children as well as adults by the score of thousands into mine, factory and workshop, there to toil for unbelievably long hours. Weekday schools kept children out of employment and were therefore bitterly opposed by industrialists. The attention of the charitable was diverted to the provision of Sunday schools, which did not interfere with employment. These sprang up like wildfire all over the country from about 1780, thanks largely to the organizing ability of Robert Raikes, a Gloucestershire pioneer of the movement who, being a newspaper proprietor, was able to give it widespread publicity.

But one-day-a-week schools, however numerous and efficient, were quite inadequate to meet the needs of a country that was fast becoming a great industrial power. This became widely recognized round the turn of the century. In 1802 Sir Robert Peel attempted (without much success) to secure for child apprentices shorter working hours and a daily period of schooling by means of his Health and Morals of Apprentices Act. In 1807 Mr Samuel Whitbread introduced into Parliament a Bill proposing a national system of Elementary schools supported from public funds. This actually got through the Commons, but was rejected by the Lords, largely because of the unyielding opposition of representatives of the Established Church. Yet at the same time both the Church of England and organized Nonconformity were on the point of becoming committed to support of voluntary societies which aimed to provide the nation with a universal system of elementary education.

Two hitherto insuperable obstacles to the provision by private charity of such a system were the formidable recurrent cost involved and the perennial scarcity of competent teachers. In the closing years of the eighteenth century two men, Dr Andrew Bell, an Anglican priest, and Joseph Lancaster, a Quaker, almost simultaneously demonstrated that both obstacles could be overcome, that elementary education could be provided at an extremely cheap rate, and involve the employment of very few adult teachers, if the simple expedient were adopted of using selected pupils to teach the others. This 'monitorial' system made an immediate appeal to the ruling classes. Money poured in, and two voluntary societies (both still in existence) were founded to stimulate the establishment of schools conducted on the lines laid down respectively by Bell and Lancaster: the National Society for Promoting the Education of the Poor in the Principles of the Established Church throughout England and Wales,[9] and the

British and Foreign School Society, the latter a body sponsoring schools on a non-denominational basis. Within twenty years members of these societies had provided, entirely out of voluntary contributions, numerous schools through-out the country. It was a remarkable achievement; nevertheless, even within this period of exceptional activity it became obvious to the discerning few that, despite the readiness with which the rich were subscribing to this charity – as they were also to others – and despite the devotion with which innumerable persons, both priests and laymen, were giving themselves to the work of establishing and maintaining schools, voluntary effort could never by itself cope with the gigantic task of schooling all the nation's children. And so the demand was pressed again and again for aid to be provided from public funds.

Finally, with success. In 1833 the House of Commons was induced to grant the sum of £20,000 to assist the National and British Societies to build schools. The grant was repeated the following year, and in 1839 was increased to £30,000. In that year the Government created an Education Committee of the Privy Council to supervise the distribution and use of what had become an annual grant, and the newly-formed Committee at once claimed the right to inspect all grant-aided schools. Such were the modest beginnings in England of State intervention in public education.

The Committee of the Privy Council on Education was singularly fortunate in its first secretary, Dr James Kay – better known as Sir James Kay-Shuttleworth. Though he held office for only ten years he laid the foundations of a system of elementary education which lasted for a hundred. He killed the 'monitorial' method of instruction by introducing a national scheme of grant-aided 'pupil-teachers', and by subsidizing training colleges. He encouraged the schools to take up many subjects and activities beyond the '3 Rs'. Not least among his great contributions was his establishment of Her Majesty's Inspectorate of Schools, and his insistence that HMI must be advisers, not dictators.

During his period of office Kay-Shuttleworth was continuously harassed by sectarian problems, by the determined antagonism of a large body of opinion (both within the Church of England and among the Nonconformists) which fiercely resented any form of State intervention in education, by the hostility of many industrialists to any extension of elementary education (which diminished their supply of cheap labour), and by the apathy of innumerable parents.

A confused struggle between warring factions persisted for many years, seriously retarding and stunting the growth and development of elementary education. Industry, aided and abetted by parents, snatched children of tender age from the schools – if, indeed, they were allowed to enter them; governmental economy scored a dreadful triumph (one only of many) when by the Revised Code of 1862 it so restricted grants as to cut the curriculum of the Elementary schools virtually to the '3 Rs'; denominational pride and prejudices frustrated any hope of a united voluntary effort; and all these forces hindering progress towards the national system of education which the country desperately needed were powerfully supported by the prevalent political and economic doctrine of *laissez-faire*, which in more brutal terms meant every man for himself, with the minimum of government, and the devil take the hindmost. The story of elementary education in England and Wales between 1833 and 1870 is not one to be proud of; its most pleasing features are the enlightened work of the early HMIs, and the undoubted heroism of many teachers, who, with the most meagre resources and almost complete lack of public support, tamed and taught great hordes of children who otherwise would have grown up half-savage and illiterate.

The first decisive advance towards a statutory system of public education was delayed until 1870; and even then the Elementary Education Act passed in that year was a typical English compromise. This Act, piloted through Parliament by W. E. Forster, in face of fierce and sustained opposition, maintained the voluntary system; but at least it empowered the Government to 'fill the gaps'. In districts where no voluntary schools existed, or where the provision of elementary education was judged inadequate, local School Boards were to be elected, with power to provide and maintain Elementary schools out of public funds. Sectarian rivalries, which had killed many previous Bills, and threatened death to this one, were at the last moment appeased by a formula which provided that in the 'Board' schools "no religious catechism or religious formulary which is distinctive of any particular denomination"[10] was to be taught. One crucially important consequence of this compromise was that it established in England and Wales a system of 'Dual Control' of elementary education, with statutory and voluntary bodies sharing the responsibility for the provision and maintenance of schools. This system has persisted, though with many modifications, down to the present day.

Though it is often incorrectly stated to have done so, the 1870 Act did not make attendance at school compulsory. It empowered School Boards to make attendance compulsory within their areas, and many did so. But to enforce compulsory attendance everywhere in 1870 would have been impossible, because in many districts the number of children of school age was far greater than the number of school places. A remarkable spurt of building, by both the voluntary societies and the School Boards, enabled the Government to introduce in 1876 a partial measure of compulsion, and to make attendance at school compulsory everywhere in 1880. In 1891 tuition fees in Public Elementary schools were largely done away with by the Government's offer to pay compensatory grants to schools which gave up charging them. Total abolition of fees in Elementary schools was not, however, effected until 1918.

While the sectarians were wrangling over the control of elementary education, reform was gradually getting under way in secondary and higher education. In part this was brought about by the efforts of individual reformers, amongst whom Thomas Arnold, headmaster of Rugby School from 1828 to 1842, and George Birkbeck, founder of the Mechanics' Institutes, rank high; in part it was the result of increasing pressure from public opinion, especially from the now powerful and wealthy middle classes.

Revolt against the Anglican exclusiveness of Oxford and Cambridge brought into being between 1828 and 1836 a University of London – of which more later. In the 1850s Royal Commissions were forced upon the ancient Universities, and consequent Acts of Parliament effected radical changes in their centuries-old constitutions. In the 1860s, other Royal Commissions investigated, first, the constitutions and curricula of the nine old and famous schools which ranked as 'public' schools,[11] and secondly all the other endowed schools, nearly 3,000 in number. These investigations also were followed by Acts of Parliament, which remodelled the constitutions of the public schools and redistributed the endowments of many of the others, in part to make provision for the secondary education of girls, which on a substantial scale dates only from the 1870s. Education for women at a higher level had begun in London in the 1840s with the founding of the Queen's and Bedford Colleges; twenty years more were to elapse before Girton College gave it a slender footing at Cambridge, and thirty before Somerville College and Lady Margaret Hall were opened at Oxford.

From the 1850s onward mounting anxiety about the increasingly successful industrial competition Great Britain was having to face from European countries,[12] and the well-founded belief that these countries were enabled to compete so successfully because they had built up efficient systems of vocational education, resulted in a spate of commissions of inquiry, both official and private. These provoked both governmental and voluntary action. In the 1850s the Government established a Department of Science and Art; in the 1870s the Corporation of the City of London with some of the City Livery Companies (the descendants of the medieval craft and merchant guilds) drew up plans for a national system of technical education and founded the City and Guilds of London Institute; in the 1880s the Government appointed a Royal Commission on Technical Instruction, and followed this up by passing in 1889 a Technical Instruction Act. This Act, the first of its kind, empowered the County and County Borough Councils (created in 1888) to spend a limited amount of public money in providing and grant-aiding vocational education. Thanks to the Act, but much more to the diversion to educational purposes of large sums from Customs and Excise and from London charities which had outlived their original purposes, the 1890s saw a rapid and substantial growth of technical colleges and evening schools providing a wide variety of vocational courses.

Liberal adult education was still left to voluntary enterprise, which was not lacking. The 1840s had seen the foundation, in Sheffield, of the first People's College, to be followed in 1854 by the famous Working Men's College (still flourishing) in north London; and in 1867 a young Cambridge don, James Stuart, started one of the country's greatest adult education movements by delivering, at the request of the newly-formed North of England Council for Promoting the Higher Education of Women, a series of public lectures in Leeds, Liverpool, Manchester, Sheffield, Rochdale and Crewe, which gave birth to 'University Extension'.

But the keystone of the educational arch was still missing. Practically every inquiry, public or private, into the state of education from the 1860s onward had emphasized the urgent need to create a national system of secondary education.

At long last, in 1894, a Royal Commission (the 'Bryce' Commission) was instructed to recommend how this could best be done. Its labours resulted, first, in an Act of Parliament, passed in 1899, which created a national Board of Education to supervise elementary, secondary and vocational education, and secondly in the epoch-making Education Act of 1902. This Act, passed in face of denominational controversy as bitter as that of 1870, made three fundamental changes in the law relating to public education. It made available to voluntary schools money from local rates as well as national taxes (that was what caused most controversy); it abolished the *ad hoc* School Boards and made the general purpose County and County Borough Councils the local authorities for education; and it empowered these councils to provide, and grant-aid the provision of, 'education other than elementary', thus making possible the long-desired statutory system of secondary education.

The 1902 Act paved the way for great advances, but it did not, alas, create a completely articulated system of public education. That was not to come until 1944. The 1902 structure was made up of two imperfectly co-ordinated parts, elementary education and 'education other than elementary', that is, all other forms of public education, including secondary education. The local education authorities (LEAs) were given fundamentally different responsibilities in respect of these two parts. They were placed under a statutory *duty* to secure the provision of adequate facilities for elementary education, but were bound by no such duty in respect of 'education other than elementary'; they were merely given permissive *powers* to provide and grant-aid the provision of this. As a result, some authorities made generous provision while others did as little as possible.

This dichotomy in the educational system was emphasized by two other factors. Pressure from vested interests had compelled the inclusion in the 1902 Act, alongside the County and County Borough Councils, of a second group of LEAs: the Councils of all non-county (municipal) boroughs having populations exceeding 10,000 at the 1901 Census and of all urban districts (i.e. town districts organized for local government but not possessing the status of borough) with populations exceeding 20,000. These minor authorities[13] were given responsibility for elementary education only; consequently, in their areas two local authorities for education might be operating, one for elementary and the other for higher education: a situation fraught with possibilities for friction, especially if one authority was progressive and the other laggard.

The other factor was that the two parts of the educational system were not made end-on to each other. Elementary education was compulsory up to the age of fourteen – nominally, but owing to a system of 'exemptions' large numbers of children left school at thirteen – and was restricted to children under sixteen. But secondary education began ordinarily at ten or eleven, and could be started earlier. The two parts thus ran parallel for several years. This could have provided a valuable opportunity for developing varied but closely co-ordinated forms of post-primary education. Unfortunately, the times were not ripe for this; the social gulf which yawned between the Public Elementary school on the one hand and the endowed and proprietary Secondary schools on the other was still too wide. What was done was to expand greatly, and systematize, the provision of scholarships enabling clever children to transfer from elementary to secondary education at about the age of eleven. In 1907 Regulations made under an Education (Administrative Provisions) Act required all Secondary schools maintained or aided by LEAs to reserve a given percentage (usually one-quarter) of their entry for pupils from Elementary schools awarded 'free places' by the LEA, which would pay their tuition fees.

In the early days many old-established Secondary schools resented the presence of 'free-placers' in their midst, but the passage of time and the ability of these pupils from Elementary schools gradually wore away the prejudice against them. A more persistent, and most unhappy, consequence of the free-place scheme was that, as the number of places available was usually much smaller than the number of candidates, many Elementary schools began systematically to coach and cram their abler pupils for what quickly became in many places a highly competitive examination.

The new system of secondary education was developed vigorously during the years preceding the First World War. Many endowed Grammar schools were accepted into it, as were some 'Higher Grade' and other senior Elementary schools which had been doing advanced work; and the LEAs established numerous new schools. Two criticisms are made of the policy pursued by the Board of Education during these years: that the curriculum of the Secondary school was assimilated too closely to the academic and literary pattern of that followed in the public and endowed Grammar schools; and that to meet the mounting demand for secondary education other parts of the educational system – notably vocational education – were starved. The criticisms are, on the whole, justified. Nevertheless, during these years there emerged two new types of post-Primary school which were later to become important elements in the structure of secondary education: the Junior Technical school, offering to pupils – mainly from Elementary schools – between the ages of twelve or thirteen and sixteen quasi-vocational courses, and the Central school – first pioneered by London and Manchester in 1911 and 1912 – a type of senior Elementary school which also offered vocationally biased courses, but not so strongly vocational as those of the Junior Technical school. The Central school recruited its pupils at eleven-plus and gave them a four-year course.

Concurrently with the building up of a statutory system of secondary education came the first large-scale creation of universities in England. For over six hundred years, from the beginning of the thirteenth century to the nineteenth, the country had two only, Oxford and Cambridge (which successfully resisted occasional attempts to found others). In the fourth decade of the nineteenth century two more were founded: Durham, a collegiate University modelled on Oxford, and London. The 'University of London' which was opened in 1828 was intended to provide university education for Nonconformists, then still excluded from the ancient Universities. The attempt immediately provoked the foundation alongside it of a rival Church of England establishment. Neither the unsectarian 'University of London' (University College, London) nor the Anglican King's College succeeded in gaining the coveted University charter, nor could any way be found of including their two dissimilar constitutions within the terms of a single charter. So, as a compromise, in 1836 an examining body called London University was created, and given power to affiliate colleges wishing to take its examinations; and an examining body only the University remained until 1900.

This unsatisfactory half-solution of an apparently insoluble problem was later to produce highly important, extremely gratifying and quite unanticipated consequences. The second half of the nineteenth century saw the rise, chiefly in large industrial cities, and generally as the result of a juncture of private enterprise and civic pride, of a number of colleges offering courses of advanced study for adults, usually with a strong bias towards the natural sciences and technology. The promoters of most of these colleges had in mind their ultimate attainment of university status; and in pursuit of this aim they found in the 'external' degrees of London University (which in 1858 were made available to students anywhere) an invaluable aid. By preparing their students for these degrees they established academic standards justifying application for a charter, first as a University College and finally as a full University. In 1880 Owens College at Manchester was incorporated into a newly created federal University, the Victoria University, to which in the next few years colleges at Leeds and Liverpool also became affiliated. In 1893 three Welsh colleges, at Aberystwyth, Bangor, and Cardiff, united forces to form a federal University of Wales. Seven years later a veritable spate of foundations began. In 1900 Mason College, Birmingham, was granted a charter, and became the University of Birmingham. Shortly afterwards the Manchester federation was dissolved, and in its place there arose the Victoria University of Manchester (1903) and the Universities of Liverpool (1903) and Leeds (1904). The University College of Sheffield, previously refused affiliation by Manchester, made good its claim to full university status in 1905, and the cycle of creation was closed by the granting of a university charter to the Bristol University College in 1908.

The First World War temporarily halted developments in all parts of the educational system, but was the cause of fresh advances. During its later years grave concern was felt for the welfare of adolescents, whose labour was being exploited by unscrupulous employers, and in 1918 an Education Act was passed which was principally designed to extend to them a larger measure of educational care and guidance. The 1918 Act raised the school-leaving age to fourteen for all, and legislated for a system of compulsory part-time education to the age of eighteen for all young people who ceased full-time education before that age. The attempt to put the latter into operation ended in failure – a failure which has not yet been remedied. The part-time system was launched in 1920, but broke down within two years owing to governmental economy, lack of adequate preparation, and widespread public opposition. Its meagre results were that a single school, at Rugby, continued to work under statutory regulations, and a small number of schools, chiefly in London, on a voluntary basis.

A much less publicized Section of the 1918 Act,[14] however, brought in its train momentous consequences. This Section laid upon the LEAs a statutory duty to provide for the older and more able pupils in Public Elementary schools courses of advanced and of practical instruction. This was the first time the Elementary school had been permitted officially to provide any education beyond elementary education. There was to be a swift sequel. In 1924 the Labour Government, representing a party which since the early years of the century had advocated a policy of 'secondary education for all', requested the Consultative Committee of the Board of Education to inquire into 'the organization, objective and curriculum of courses of study' suitable for children remaining at schools other than Grammar schools up to the age of fifteen. The result was the famous 'Hadow' Report (so called from the name of the chairman of the Committee, Sir W. H. Hadow) on *The Education of the Adolescent*,[15] a major landmark in modern English education.

The seminal recommendation made by the Committee was that at about the age of eleven the first, or primary, stage of education should be concluded and a new stage begun, which for all children should be regarded as secondary education. To implement the recommendation the Committee proposed the division of the Public Elementary school into two schools: a Junior, or Primary, school for pupils up to the age of eleven, and a Senior, or Secondary, school for pupils beyond that age. The latter, they suggested, might be called the 'Modern' school. The Committee also recommended that the period of compulsory full-time education be extended to fifteen. That was not done, but 'Hadow reorganization' of the Elementary school was made national policy. The responsibility for carrying it out lay with the LEAs, who acted with varying enthusiasm and speed. By the outbreak of the Second World War roughly two-thirds of all Elementary schools had been reorganized. In general, reorganization was much more advanced in urban than in rural areas, and the majority of the unreorganized schools were voluntary schools, many of which found the cost prohibitive.

The 'Hadow' committee was unwilling to grant the title 'Secondary' to Junior Technical and comparable schools providing vocationally biased courses, regarding them as giving not secondary but vocational education. A later report by the Consultative Committee, the 'Spens' Report (chairman, Sir W. Spens), in 1938[16] took a different view. It recognized that many of these schools had liberalized their curricula and were, in effect, giving a general education. So by the outbreak of the Second World War the stage was set both for acceptance of the idea of 'secondary education for all' and for its development along the three broad lines of Grammar, Modern, and Technical education.

The causes which evoked a widespread and clamant demand for radical reform of the English educational system during the early years of the Second World War are extremely complex. But almost certainly the habits and behaviour of some of the mothers and children evacuated in 1939 from slum areas was the spark that set off the conflagration, for they revealed the fact that children were still being brought up in ignorant and sordid fashion. And with true instinct public opinion realized that the key to the cure of this was better education.

By 1940 teachers and social workers were clamouring for reform. The Board of Education reacted promptly, and in 1941 sent to numerous bodies, both statutory and voluntary, a document (the 'Green Book')[17] which contained numerous proposals and invited suggestions, comments, and criticisms. The response was almost overwhelming; a veritable avalanche of detailed replies poured into the Board (many being simultaneously published by their authors), and the President, Mr R. A. (now Lord) Butler, and his Parliamentary Secretary, Mr J. Chuter Ede, were for many months kept in continuous consultation with all sorts of bodies directly or indirectly concerned. It quickly became apparent that about purely educational reforms there was little substantial difference of opinion; what took much more time was reaching an agreement with the Churches about the future position of voluntary schools.

In July 1943 Mr Butler presented to Parliament a 'White Paper', entitled *Educational Reconstruction*, which set out the Government's proposed reforms. Following discussion of these he introduced into Parliament in December 1943 a Bill which on 3rd August the following year became law as the Education Act 1944. Unlike previous Education Bills, this one provoked little denominational or other serious controversy; there were during its passage through the Houses of Parliament clashes of opinion about various matters, but no fundamental reform embodied in the Bill was challenged. This was in part due to the fact that the Government was a coalition commanding the support of all the political parties, in part to the exhaustive consultations which had preceded the introduction of the Bill, and in part to the great weight of public opinion behind the reforms proposed.

The 1944 Act reorganized drastically the statutory system of public education in England and Wales. The main changes it made may be summarized as follows:

1. The President of the Board of Education, with his limited power of 'superintendence' of public education, was replaced by a Minister of Education with a statutory duty to "promote the education of the people of England and Wales" and to "secure the effective execution, by local authorities under his control and direction, of the national policy for providing a varied and comprehensive educational service in every area".

2. (*a*) The County and County Borough Councils were made the sole local authorities for education. The 'Part III Authorities' ceased to exist, but provision was made for delegating limited powers in counties to 'divisional executives' in charge of specified areas.

(*b*) The LEAs were made statutorily responsible for securing adequate facilities in their areas for all forms of public education.

3. (*a*) The statutory system of public education was reorganized in three progressive stages: *Primary* (age five to eleven–plus), *Secondary* (twelve to eighteen plus), and *Further* education, comprising all forms of education except

full-time secondary, and university education, for persons beyond 'compulsory school age'.

(*b*) Compulsion to receive full-time education began, as previously, at the age of five, but the Act required the LEAs to have particular regard to the need to provide Nursery schools and classes for children under the age of five. It raised immediately the upper limit of 'compulsory school age' from fourteen to fifteen, and made provision for a later raising to sixteen.

(*c*) Tuition fees were abolished in all secondary schools maintained by LEAs.

4. Voluntary schools were give the choice of becoming 'aided' or 'controlled' schools. As 'aided' schools they would retain the right to give denominational religious instruction, to conduct denominational religious worship, and (subject to certain conditions) to appoint their teachers. In return they had to accept responsibility for meeting half the cost of any structural improvements to their premises required by the LEA. As 'controlled' schools they would have no financial responsibilities whatever, all these being taken over by the LEA; but they surrendered the right to hold denominational religious worship on the school premises, and to give denominational religious instruction, except during a maximum of two school periods a week to the children of parents who desired it. In both cases the Board of Managers (Primary schools) or Governors (Secondary schools) retained ownership of the school premises.

Provision was also made for a third category, of 'Special Agreement' schools. Under the Education Act 1936 the government had, in order to speed up Hadow reorganization, offered large grants towards the building of voluntary Secondary schools. Of the agreements made, some 500 had not been implemented before the outbreak of war in 1939. These could be taken up on the same terms as previously. Special Agreement schools would have a status closely resembling that of voluntary aided schools.

5. A daily act of corporate religious worship and regular and systematic religious instruction were made compulsory in all Primary and Secondary schools maintained by LEAs. In 'county' schools (i.e., those provided by the LEA) and voluntary controlled schools the religious instruction (other than the two periods a week in 'controlled' schools) was to be in accordance with an 'Agreed Syllabus' compiled or adopted for each area by a statutory committee representative of the LEA, the teachers, and the Churches concerned.

6. All independent schools were, from a date to be specified, to be registered with the Ministry of Education. After that date it would be a legal offence to open or conduct an unregistered school. The Minister was given power, subject to appeal, to require improvement of sub-standard independent schools and to close inefficient or inadequately equipped schools.

7. (*a*) The LEAs were statutorily required to secure, in addition to medical inspection, free medical (including dental) treatment for all pupils between the ages of two and eighteen in maintained schools, and other maintained educational establishments.

(*b*) The LEAs were required to provide "milk, meals and other refreshment for pupils in attendance at schools and county colleges maintained by them".

They were empowered to provide necessitous children with clothing, and any children with clothing for physical training. If circumstances demanded they could provide children with board and lodging.

Any independent school could make arrangements with the LEA to participate in the School Health Service and the School Milk and Meals Services.

8. The LEAs were required to have particular regard to the needs of children suffering from "any disability of mind or body". They had to ascertain what children in their areas required special educational treatment because of such disability, and to provide for them appropriate educational treatment.

9. Both the Minister of Education and the LEAs were empowered, "for the purpose of enabling pupils to take advantage without hardship to themselves or their parents of any educational facilities available to them",

(a) to defray expenses of children attending maintained schools,

(b) to pay fees and other expenses for children attending fee-paying schools, and

(c) to grant scholarships and other awards to pupils over compulsory school age.

10. (a) The LEAs were required to secure the provision of adequate facilities not only for formal education for persons over compulsory school age, but also for "leisure time occupation in organized cultural training and recreative activities".

(b) The LEAs were required to provide, after a date to be specified, a compulsory system of part-time education for all young persons up to the age of eighteen not in full-time secondary education or some other officially recognized form of full- or part-time education. This part-time education was to be conducted in 'County Colleges' and to occupy the equivalent of one day a week.

11. The LEAs were required to pay teachers in maintained schools and colleges according to salary scales agreed by the 'Burnham Committee' (the statutory negotiating body, representative of the teachers and their employers, the LEAs), and approved by the Minister.

12. No woman having professional qualifications to teach could be debarred from taking a teaching post, or be dismissed from one, for the sole reason that she was married.

The Act received the Royal Assent on 3 August 1944. Part I, which deals with central administration, and Part V (supplementary provisions, many to do with bringing the Act into operation), came into effect at once. Part II (organization of the statutory system) and Part IV (miscellaneous provisions) came into operation on 1 April 1945, except that the raising of the school-leaving age from 14 to 15 was delayed until 1 April 1947. Part III (Independent schools) came into operation on 30 September 1957. The school-leaving age was raised to 16 on 1 September 1972. Compulsory part-time further education in County Colleges had not been brought into operation by the end of 1976.

Since the passing of the 1944 Act (the 'Principal' Act) many of its Sections have been modified; up to December 1976 by nearly twenty 'amending' Acts,[18] and by various other Acts of Parliament. Particularly important among the latter are the London Government Act 1963, the Local Government Act 1972, the Employment and Training Act 1973, and the National Health Service Reorganisation Act 1973. None of the changes made has undermined the basic educational principles on which the 1944 Act was built, but several (among both amending and other Acts) have made substantial alterations in organizational or financial arrangements. For example, the Education Act 1964 gave LEAs and voluntary bodies the power to establish Primary and Secondary schools within different age limits from those laid down in the 1944 Act – and thus brought into being a new kind of school, the 'Middle' school. Three amending Acts progressively reduced the level of the contribution towards capital expenditure on school buildings due from the managers or governors of voluntary aided and special agreement schools: the Education Act 1959 from 50 per cent to 25 per cent, the Education Act 1967 from 25 per cent to 20 per cent, and the Education Act 1975 from 20 per cent to 15 per cent. The Education Act 1976 gave the Secretary of State power to compel LEAs to organize their secondary schools on comprehensive lines.

The London Government Act 1963 created the Inner London Education Authority (ILEA), an LEA that is neither a County nor a County Borough Council. The Local Government Act 1972 reorganized drastically the structure of local government throughout England and Wales, except in the Greater London area (reorganized by the 1963 Act), and the Isles of Scilly. It replaced the hierarchy of County and County Borough, Municipal Borough, and Urban and Rural Districts, by a simpler pattern of Metropolitan and Non-Metropolitan Counties, each divided into Districts. In Metropolitan Counties the councils of the Districts are the LEAs, in Non-Metropolitan Counties the councils of the Counties.

The Employment and Training Act 1973 abolished the Youth Employment service (YES), which had been optional for LEAs (though most undertook it), and laid upon LEAs a statutory duty to provide a Careers Service, available to all pupils and students (of whatever age) in attendance at maintained schools or colleges. The National Health Service Reorganisation Act 1973 transferred the responsibility for the School Health Service from the LEAs to Area Health Authorities (AHAs) working under the direction of the Secretary of State for Health and Social Security. Three years previously the Education (Handicapped Children) Act 1970 had transferred responsibility for the education of 'severely subnormal' children (ESN/S) from the Department of Health and Social Security (DHSS) to the Department of Education and Science (DES).

Some Developments since 1944

During the quarter of a century between 1944 and 1970 the English educational system was expanded and altered on a scale unprecedented in its history. The following paragraphs note some of the more outstanding items; further information is given in relevant chapters.

Three months before the Education Act 1944 was passed, the Report was published of a committee, under the chairmanship of Sir Arnold (later Lord) McNair, Vice-Chancellor of Liverpool University, which had been appointed in 1942 "to consider the Supply, Recruitment and Training of Teachers and Youth Leaders".[19] One-half of this committee of ten persons recommended that the universities should accept full responsibility for the education and training of teachers. By 1951 all except three universities – Cambridge, Liverpool, Reading – had done so, and by 1955 Liverpool and Reading had also accepted full responsibility.

Between 1945 and 1951 an Emergency Training scheme added some 35,000 Qualified Teachers to a teaching force (in maintained schools) which in 1946–47 was under 200,000 strong. By 1951 the annual output of teachers from the permanent training establishments had been increased to about double what it was in 1938. During the 1960s the rate of increase was greatly accelerated, so that by 1970 the output was five times that of 1938.

Between 1945 and 1970 over 12,000 new maintained Primary and Secondary schools were built, with accommodation for about two-thirds of the children attending LEA schools. Many were attractively designed and equipped, and some were highly experimental; notably, the 'open plan' Primary schools.

From the early 1950s the sharply segregated 'tripartite' organization of secondary education in Grammar, Modern, and Technical schools, with which the country started out in 1945, was beginning to break down. Secondary Modern schools developed academic courses. Schools of different types amalgamated to form 'Bilateral' schools (e.g. Grammar-Modern), 'Multilateral', and 'Comprehensive' schools. The number of Comprehensive schools began to grow appreciably in the early 1960s, and rapidly from 1965, when a Labour Government 'requested' all LEAs to organize their secondary schools on Comprehensive lines.[20] The request was revoked by a Conservative Government in 1970,[21] but by then there were already about 1,200 Comprehensive schools, housing about one-third of the pupils in maintained Secondary schools. When the Labour Party returned to power in 1974 it re-affirmed its policy of compulsory Comprehensive education.[22] By the end of 1975 there were some 3,300 Comprehensive schools, and in them about 55 per cent of the children attending maintained Secondary schools.

Innovations designed to extend the range and improve the quality of the education given in Primary and Secondary schools included the introduction of television services by both the British Broadcasting Corporation (BBC) and the Independent Television Authority (ITA) in 1957; the launching in the 1960s of large-scale research and development in curricular studies, notably by the Schools Council for the Curriculum and Examinations (the Schools Council), which was created in 1964 by the DES, the LEAs, and the teachers' professional associations; the starting in 1965 of a new external examination, for a Certificate of Secondary Education (CSE), intended for children in the middle ranges of intellectual ability; and increasing use of a wide range of sophisticated audio-visual aids: films, film-strips, cassettes, tape-recorders, overhead projectors, language laboratories, and so on.

Proportionately, the largest expansion – and the most extensive changes – took place in Further Education (FE). Underlying both expansion and change was the transformation of FE from a mainly part-time evening occupation to one in which full-time and part-time day studies occupied an increasingly large role. Concurrently, a distinction began to be drawn between 'Further' and 'Higher' education. This distinction was officially recognized in 1956, when the structure of technical education was remodelled, with the colleges graded on four levels according to the standard of the studies which they undertook.

In 1963 the 'Robbins' Committee,[23] appointed in 1961 "to review the pattern of full-time higher education in Great Britain", and to advise on its long-term development, recommended that the ten top-level technical colleges, the 'Colleges of Advanced Technology' (CATs), should be made universities. This was done in 1966–67. Another of the Committee's recommendations proposed a Council for National Academic Awards (CNAA), to grant degrees and other qualifications to students in non-university institutions. The CNAA was created, by Royal Charter, in 1964. In 1965 a Labour Secretary of State for Education and Science, Mr Anthony Crosland, advocated in a public speech at Woolwich a 'binary' system of Higher Education which would comprise an 'autonomous' sector (the universities) and a 'public' sector (non-university institutions). He followed this up in 1966 with a White Paper entitled *A Plan for Polytechnics and Other Colleges,*[24] which envisaged a new top-level group of some 30 non-university institutions of Higher Education. By 1973 all the 30 new-style 'Polytechnics' had been created, chiefly by amalgamating two or more existing colleges.

In 1969 the report of a *Committee on Technician Courses and Examinations* (the 'Haslegrave' Report) investigated the second level of studies. It recommended that the Secretary of State should establish a Technician Education Council (TEC) and a Business Education Council (BEC), "to plan, co-ordinate and administer national technician and comparable examinations and qualifications in the technical and business sectors respectively".[25] The report also recommended the "phased introduction" of unified national patterns of courses, below the level of first degrees, in the technical and business sectors, to replace the existing pattern of City and Guilds and National Certificate and Diploma courses and examinations. The TEC was set up in 1973 and the BEC in 1974. In 1973 the TEC announced that its first courses, for a Certificate and a Diploma, would start in September 1976. In 1976 the BEC said its courses, also for Certificates and Diplomas, would start in 1977.

During the later 1960s there arose a widespread demand for a thorough investigation of the education and training of teachers. This provoked three inquiries: by a Select Committee of the House of Commons, by the ATOs at the request of Mr Edward Short, Secretary of State for Education and Science, and, somewhat later, by a Committee of Inquiry appointed by his successor, Mrs Margaret Thatcher, under the chairmanship of Lord James of Rusholme, Vice-Chancellor of York University. The 'James' Report, published in January 1972,[26] proposed a radically new scheme of teacher education and training. The

Government accepted some only of its recommendations, but less than a year later proposed equally revolutionary changes in a White Paper, *Education: A Framework for Expansion*.[27] This suggested the incorporation of many, if not most, of the training colleges into the 'public' sector of Higher Education by amalgamation with Polytechnics or other colleges. In August 1975 the DES said that the futures of over 110 Colleges of Education had been settled; but subsequent projections of the future school population showing that fewer teachers would be needed nullified this. The reorganization was still not completed at the end of 1976.

Between 1948 and 1967 the number of universities in England was almost trebled, and the number of university students more than quadrupled. The five existing university colleges[28] were upgraded. An experimental University College of North Staffordshire, opened in 1950, became in 1962 the University of Keele. In 1963 the Newcastle upon Tyne division of Durham University was made a university in its own right. Between 1961 and 1965 seven entirely new universities were created.[29] In 1966 and 1967 eight of the CATs became universities.[30] In January 1971 an entirely novel institution, the 'Open University', began work. Catering for home-based students, it teaches by means of correspondence courses and radio and television broadcasts, supplemented by seminars at local centres and national summer schools.

Three causes were principally responsible for the expansion between 1944 and 1970: the widening of opportunity by the 1944 Act; a continuously increasing school population; and a growing demand for education, especially further and higher education, based on the belief – widespread throughout the world – that upon education depended a nation's prosperity, if not survival.

From about 1970, however, it was to be a different story. Economic depression cut supplies severely. Demand for higher education slackened, in part because belief in its economic potential began to wane. The increase in the school population lessened, the birth-rate having started to fall in 1964; consequently the number of men and women accepted for training as teachers was progressively reduced.

References

1 The Seven Liberal Arts were divided into two groups. Grammar, rhetoric, and dialectic made up the *Trivium*, which was first studied, and arithmetic, geometry, astronomy, and music (a study very different from that of today; mainly number and plain song) the *Quadrivium*. Mastery of these seven arts fitted the student to embark upon the study of philosophy, and of theology, "the queen of the sciences" – that is, of knowledge.

2 From the foundation Deed of Winchester College, 1382, as translated by A. F. Leach in *Educational Charters and Documents 598 to 1909*. Cambridge University Press, 1911, p. 321.

3 Quoted from the author's *Schools of Medieval England*. Methuen, 1915, p. 206.

4 How 'indigent' candidates had to be to qualify for free places has been endlessly

disputed. See, for example, *The Public Schools and the General Educational System* (the 'Fleming' Report), HMSO, 1944, p. 8.

5 Education having as its principal aim literacy in the English language.

6 See particularly Jordan, W. K., *Philanthropy in England 1480–1660*. Allen and Unwin, 1959.

7 Jordan, op. cit., p. 286.

8 ibid., p. 291.

9 Now 'The National Society for Promoting Religious Education'.

10 Elementary Education Act 1870, Section 14 (2).

11 Charterhouse, Eton, Harrow, Merchant Taylors, Rugby, St Paul's, Shrewsbury, Westminster, Winchester. The Public Schools Act 1868, which ensued from the Commission's report, dealt only with the seven boarding schools, and not with Merchant Taylors and St Paul's.

12 Austria, Belgium, France, Prussia, and Switzerland in particular.

13 These minor authorities became known popularly as the 'Part Three' authorities, because the provisions relating to Elementary education were contained in Part III of the Act. During the greater part of the period 1902–1944 there were 169 of them, as against 146 major authorities.

14 Education Act 1918, Section 2 (I)(a).

15 HMSO, 1926.

16 *Secondary Education, with Special Reference to Grammar Schools and Technical High Schools*. HMSO, 1938.

17 The 'Green Book' was so named from the colour of its cover.

18 Education Act 1946; Education (Miscellaneous Provisions) Act 1948; Education (Miscellaneous Provisions) Act 1953; Education Act 1959; Education Act 1962; Education Act 1964; Remuneration of Teachers Act 1965; Education Act 1967; Education (No. 1) Act 1968; Education (No. 2) Act 1968; Education (School Milk) Act 1970; Education (Handicapped Children) Act 1970; Education Act 1973; Education (Work Experience) Act 1973; Education Act 1975; Education Act 1976.

19 *Teachers and Youth Leaders*. HMSO, 1944.

20 Circular 10/65, *The Organisation of Secondary Education*, dated 12 July 1965.

21 Circular 10/70, *The Organisation of Secondary Education*, dated 30 June 1970.

22 Circular 4/74, *The Organisation of Secondary Education*, dated 16 April 1974.

23 The 'Robbins' Committee was appointed by the Prime Minister, Mr Harold Macmillan. The chairman was Professor Lord Robbins.

24 Cmnd. 3006. HMSO, 1966.

25 *Education and Science in 1969*. HMSO, 1970, p. 50.

26 *Teacher Education and Training*. HMSO, 1972.

27 Cmnd. 5174. HMSO, 1972.

28 Exeter, Hull, Leicester, Nottingham, Southampton.

29 Sussex, East Anglia, York, Essex, Lancaster, Kent, Warwick.

30 Royal Technical College, Salford; Bradford Institute of Technology; Loughborough College of Technology; Birmingham College of Technology (University of Aston); Battersea Polytechnic (University of Surrey); Northampton (London) Polytechnic (City University); Merchant Venturers College, Bristol (University of Bath); Brunel College of Technology. The other two CATS, Chelsea Polytechnic and Cardiff College of Technology, became constituent colleges of, respectively, the Universities of London and Wales.

Further Reading

ADAMSON, J. W., *English Education 1789–1902*. Cambridge University Press, 1930. Reprinted 1964.

ARCHER, R. L., *Secondary Education in the Nineteenth Century*. Cambridge University Press, 1921. Reprinted by Cass, 1966.

ARGLES, MICHAEL, *South Kensington to Robbins*: An Account of English Technical and Scientific Education since 1851. Longmans, 1964.

ARMYTAGE, W. H. G., *Four Hundred Years of English Education*. Cambridge University Press, 2nd edition, 1970.

BARNARD, H. C., *A History of English Education from 1760*. University of London Press, 2nd edition, 6th impression, 1969.

BIRCHENOUGH, C., *History of Elementary Education in England and Wales from 1800 to the Present Day*. University Tutorial Press, 3rd edition, 1938.

BURGESS, H. J., *Enterprise in Education*: The story of the work of the Established Church in the education of the people prior to 1870. National Society and SPCK, 1958.

CARDWELL, D. S. L., *The Organization of Science in England*. Heinemann, Revised edition, 1972.

CURTIS, S. J., *History of Education in Great Britain*. University Tutorial Press, 7th edition, 1967.

DENT, H. C., *1870–1970, Century of Growth in English Education*. Longmans, 1970.

EVANS, KEITH, *The Development and Structure of the English Educational System*. University of London Press, 1975.

GOSDEN, P. H. J. H., *Education in the Second World War*. Methuen, 1976.

HARRISON, J. F. C., *Learning and Living 1790–1960*: A Study in the History of the Adult Education Movement. Routledge & Kegan Paul, 1961.

HURT, JOHN, *Education in Evolution*: Church, State, Society and Popular Education 1800–1870. Hart-Davis, 1971, and Paladin, 1972.

JORDAN, W. K., *Philanthropy in England 1480–1660*. Allen & Unwin, 1960.

KELLY, THOMAS, *A History of Adult Education in Great Britain*. Liverpool University Press, 2nd edition 1970.

LOWNDES, G. A. N., *The Silent Social Revolution*: An account of the expansion of Public Education in England and Wales 1895–1965. Oxford University Press, 1969.

MACLURE, J. STUART, *Educational Documents, England and Wales 1816–1967*. Methuen, 2nd edition, 1971.

MOUNTFORD, SIR JAMES, *British Universities*. Oxford University Press, 1966.

OGILVIE, VIVIAN, *The English Public School*. Batsford, 1957.

RICH, R. W., *The Training of Teachers in England and Wales during the Nineteenth Century*. Cambridge University Press, 1933. Reprinted by Chivers (Bath), 1972.

SIMON, BRIAN, *Studies in the History of Education 1780–1870* (1960); *Education and the Labour Movement 1870–1918* (1965); *The Politics of Educational Reform 1920–1940* (1974). All from Lawrence & Wishart.

SIMON, JOAN, *The Social Origins of English Education*. Routledge & Kegan Paul, 1970.

SMITH, FRANK, *A History of English Elementary Education 1760–1902*. University of London Press, 1931.

STEWART, W. A. C. and MCCANN, W. P., *The Educational Innovators 1750–1880*. Macmillan, 1967.

STEWART, W. A. C., *The Educational Innovators,* Vol. II: Progressive Schools 1881–1967. Macmillan, 1968.

STURT, MARY, *The Education of the People*: A history of primary education in England and Wales in the nineteenth century. Routledge & Kegan Paul, 1967.

WHITBREAD, NANETTE, *The Evolution of the Nursery-Infant School.* Routledge & Kegan Paul, 1972.

Official
Board of Education Consultative Committee
  The Education of the Adolescent, 1926
  The Primary School, 1931
  Infant and Nursery Schools, 1933
  Secondary Education with Special Reference to Grammar Schools and Technical High Schools, 1938
Ministry of Education, *Education 1900–1950* (annual report for 1950). HMSO, 1951.
University Grants Committee, *University Development.* Reports under this title are published every five years.

CHAPTER 2 | # Bird's Eye View

This chapter, which briefly surveys the provision of education in England and Wales, is intended as an introduction to the more detailed studies of the various parts contained in the following chapters.

There are in the United Kingdom three separate and distinct statutory systems of public education: for England and Wales, Scotland, and Northern Ireland respectively. It is the British Government's policy that these three systems shall offer approximately similar educational opportunities and maintain approximately similar educational standards, but that they shall also preserve the traditions and reflect the ethos of the peoples they serve. The three systems are regulated by separate Acts of Parliament, and are separately financed and administered.

This book deals only with education in England and Wales. As Wales is the home of a people as different from the English as are the Scots, it might logically be expected to have its own educational system. This is not the case; but since November 1970 responsibility for Primary and Secondary education in Wales has lain with the Secretary of State for Wales.[1] Further education remains the responsibility of the Secretary of State for Education and Science. A Welsh Education Office in Cardiff, under the direction of the Permanent Secretary for Welsh Education, handles the business of both Secretaries of State.

Ultimate responsibility for the statutory system of public education in England and Wales lies with the British Parliament. This enacts legislation determining the national policy for education and directing how the statutory system shall be organized, controlled and administered, provides from national funds the greater part of the money for its support, and by members' questions and occasional debates maintains a general supervision of its working. Except that the present law requires that religious instruction shall be given in all maintained Primary and Secondary schools, Parliament does not lay down what subjects shall be taught; nor does it give any directions about teaching methods, or prescribe any textbooks. These matters are held to be the business of the teacher.

Central and Local Government

The system is at the time of writing (March 1977) regulated by the Education Act 1944, as amended by subsequent Education and other Acts of Parliament. This Act entrusts the responsibility for the 'control and direction' of the statutory system to a Minister of Education. Until 1964 this Minister had charge of a single Ministry of Education, and was concerned solely with the statutory system of public education in England and Wales. On 1 April 1964 all the functions of the Minister of Education, and of the Minister of Science, were transferred to a Secretary of State for Education and Science,[2] who in addition to his responsibilities for Primary, Secondary, and Further education in England and Wales was given also responsibilities in respect of the universities and civil science throughout Great Britain.

The Secretary of State, like the Minister previously, must be a Member of Parliament, is *ex officio* a senior Minister of the Crown, and has since 1944 almost invariably been a member of the Cabinet. As the political head of the educational system the Secretary of State is held solely and personally responsible to Parliament for its administration; but by a tradition which has become impregnably established during the present century he does not directly intervene in matters of curriculum or teaching method, though, as will become apparent in subsequent chapters, there are various means whereby he can, and does, exert influence on such matters.

The Secretary of State is assisted in his Parliamentary and Departmental duties by Ministers of State and Parliamentary Under-Secretaries of State. The numbers of each tend to vary with different Governments; in 1968, for example, there were three Ministers of State and one Under-Secretary, in December 1975 one Minister of State, and one Under-Secretary. All must be members of Parliament (Commons *or* Lords), and all have Ministerial rank. Ordinarily, each will be given specific responsibilities, e.g. Minister of State for Higher Education. The Department of Education and Science (DES) is a normal Government department, staffed by Civil Servants and a corps of Her Majesty's Inspectors of Schools (HMIs). It is primarily concerned with the creation, interpretation, execution, and supervision of national policy as laid down in Acts of Parliament and Regulations made under these Acts. The DES does not provide or maintain any schools or colleges, or employ, pay, or dismiss any teachers; these matters are the responsibility of the universities, the LEAs, or the governing bodies of independent establishments. Nor does the DES prescribe, or in any way control, the supply, or influence the character of, text and other books used in schools, colleges or universities.

The structure of local government in England and Wales was drastically reorganized by the Local Government Act 1972, which came into operation on 1 April 1974. Between 1944 and 1974 the LEAs were the Councils of the administrative counties (which were rather more numerous than the geographical ones), and of the County Boroughs, that is, cities and towns that had been granted by Royal Charter the status of County Borough. From 1944 to 1964 there were 146 LEAs; 129 in England and 17 in Wales. Subsequent reorganizations in the Greater London area and elsewhere had before 1974 raised the number to 164.

Under the Local Government Act 1972 the areas of all except five of the counties were altered, new counties were created, some of the old ones disappeared, and the County Boroughs were absorbed into the new Counties. These are of two kinds: Metropolitan and Non-Metropolitan. Both kinds are divided into Districts. (The *Divisions* into which the former Counties might be divided were abolished.)

There are six Metropolitan Counties, all in England, and 47 Non-Metropolitan, of which 39 are in England and eight in Wales. In the Metropolitan Counties the councils of the *Districts* are the LEAs, in the Non-Metropolitan the councils of the *Counties*. The Greater London area, which had been reorganized in 1965, was not altered; nor were the Isles of Scilly. So from 1 April 1974 the LEAs in England and Wales have been:

47 Non-Metropolitan County Councils
36 Metropolitan County District Councils
20 Outer London Borough Councils
 1 Inner London Education Authority (ILEA)

The statutory powers and duties of LEAs were very little altered by the Local Government Act. The Education Committee remained a statutory committee, despite strong opposition while the Bill was being debated; the provision laid down in the Education Act 1944 that every LEA must "establish such education committees as they think it expedient to establish for the efficient discharge of their functions with respect to education,"[3] still holds. As previously, no LEA may make a policy decision about its educational service without having considered a report on the matter from its Education Committee. Every LEA must still appoint a Chief Education Officer (CEO), but it need no longer submit a short list of candidates for the Secretary of State's approval.

An important change was made by the National Health Service Reorganisation Act 1973, which transferred, as from 1 April 1974, the responsibility for the School Health Service from the LEAs to Area Health Authorities (AHAs) working under the control and direction of the Secretary of State for Health and Social Security. The providing of suitable premises for the new Service, and the ascertainment of handicapped children remained LEA responsibilities, but all medical and dental staff are provided by the AHAs.

The Employment and Training Act 1973, which also came into operation on 1 April 1974, made it the statutory duty of all LEAs to provide a Careers Service, which would include advice, training, and placing in employment, for all persons attending, whether full-time or part-time, educational institutions – universities excepted.

Finance

The statutory system of public education is financed by:

(a) Money voted by Parliament, and distributed to local authorities. This money comes from the revenue raised by national taxation.

(*b*) Money voted by local authorities, and disbursed by them. This money comes from the rates, that is, the local tax which each authority is empowered to levy within its area.

(*c*) Endowments, gifts (in cash or in kind), FE and university students' fees, and contributions required by law from voluntary bodies in respect of capital expenditure on buildings provided by them.

The amounts contributed from sources (*a*) and (*b*) constitute all but a relatively very small part of the total amount of the money expended on the educational system.

Up to the financial year 1958–59 (ended 31 March 1959) the respective amounts of money coming from sources (*a*) and (*b*) were calculated on a percentage basis, the central Government contributing approximately 60 per cent, and the LEAs approximately 40 per cent. From the year 1959–60 (beginning 1 April 1959) the Government began to make general, or 'block', grants to the local authorities for all purposes of local government, and from that date it became the responsibility of the local authorities to determine how much of the resources available to them should be expended on public education. Under the Local Government Act 1966, which came into operation on 1 April 1967, the block grant is termed the 'Rate Support Grant' (RSG), and is made up of three elements: two based on assessment of the LEAs' 'needs' and 'resources', and a small direct subsidy called the 'domestic' element. The RSG for 1976–77 amounted to 65.5 per cent of the local authorities' relevant expenditure.

The annual estimates of expenditure made by the local authorities include both capital and current expenditure. Capital expenditure is, however, normally financed by long-term loans, and consequently only loan charges are included in the estimates.

Teachers' salaries constitute the largest item in the educational budget. All teachers serving in schools and colleges maintained by LEAs are employed and paid by the authorities, but their rates of pay are fixed by national agreements. These agreements are made, each for a stated period, by statutory committees, each consisting of two panels representing, on the one side the DES and the LEAs, and on the other the teachers' professional organizations. There is one committee for Primary and Secondary schools (the Burnham[4] Main Committee), and one for Further Education establishments (the Burnham Further and Higher Education Committee). Agreements made by these committees have to be submitted to the Secretary of State. When he has approved an agreement all LEAs are legally obliged to pay the rates it specifies.

The Statutory System

The statutory system of public education was arranged by the 1944 Act in three progressive stages:

1 PRIMARY EDUCATION, from the age of five to between eleven and twelve.

This could be preceded by Nursery education (voluntary) between the ages of two and five.

2 SECONDARY EDUCATION, from 11–12 to 18. Compulsory until 15 (or, when judged practicable, until 16), but available (voluntary) until the 19th birthday.

3 FURTHER EDUCATION, available to all persons of all ages beyond 'compulsory school age'.

The Education Act 1964 empowered LEAs, or other persons, to submit proposals to the Secretary of State for the establishment by them of Primary and Secondary schools admitting pupils below the age of $10\frac{1}{2}$ years (the minimum age for transfer from Primary to Secondary, fixed by the Education Act 1948), and retaining them beyond the age of 12. The result was the 'Middle' school, which admits pupils at eight, nine, or ten, and keeps them until 12, 13, or 14. A Middle school can be 'deemed' Primary or Secondary.

No tuition fees may be charged for Primary and Secondary education given in schools maintained by LEAs. As Further education is voluntary, tuition fees are charged, but these are usually remitted for students aged 16–18.

While the facilities provided by the statutory system are available to all, no one is compelled by law to make use of them. There is no legal compulsion upon parents to send their children to school; the Education Act 1944 expressly states (Section 36) that children may be educated "at school or otherwise". The legal obligation upon the parent, or guardian, is to ensure that during the years of compulsion their children receive "efficient full-time education suitable to their age, ability, and aptitude". Actually, almost all children are sent to school. Because of the rapid growth of Middle schools, and the reorganization of secondary education on Comprehensive lines, the numbers of schools of different kinds, and of pupils in each kind, are continuously changing. Consequently, the following statistics will need frequent updating.

In January 1976 there were 8,492,000 children in 26,120 Primary, Middle, and Secondary schools maintained by LEAs. Of these children 4,792,000 were in 21,390 Primary schools (including Middle schools 'deemed Primary'), and 3,700,000 in 4,730 Secondary schools (including Middle schools 'deemed Secondary'). There were about 1,150 Middle schools (rather more Secondary than Primary), with over 400,000 children.

For children between the ages of two and five there were about 600 Nursery schools, and a much larger number of Nursery classes in Primary schools. In these schools and classes about 45,000 children were attending full-time, and over 100,000 attending part-time. For handicapped children there were over 1,600 Special schools, including hospital schools, with about 140,000 children. Most of these schools were provided by LEAs.

The Primary schools were staffed by 199,900 teachers, the Secondary by about 217,300 (in both cases these figures include the full-time equivalent of relatively small numbers of part-time teachers). Except for a few employed temporarily, all were Qualified Teachers. The pupil–teacher ratios were:

Primary, 24.0, Secondary, 17.0. In Special schools there were about 16,000 teachers; pupil–teacher ratios differed fairly widely.

Not maintained by LEAs, but receiving grant from the DES, were about 320 'Direct Grant' schools. Of these 174 were Secondary Grammar schools; to these payment of grant from the DES ceased in 1976.[5] By the end of 1975 over 100 had decided to become Independent schools, and 51 (most of them Roman Catholic schools) to be maintained by LEAs.

Not in receipt of any grant from public funds were rather more than 2,000 Independent schools. Of these about 1,400, with around 350,000 pupils, were 'Recognized as Efficient' by the DES. The others – a rapidly decreasing group – had considerably under 100,000 pupils, three-quarters of them of Primary school age.

Further Education

Maintained or grant-aided[6] by LEAs were 30 Polytechnics, about 550 other major establishments (Colleges or Institutes of Higher Education, Colleges of Further Education, Colleges of Art and Design, and other more specialized colleges), and nearly 7,000 Evening Institutes. In 1975 these were attended by about $3\frac{1}{4}$ million students, of whom about $\frac{1}{4}$ million were full time (including 'sandwich'), and about $\frac{3}{4}$ million part-time day. There were also four direct-grant colleges[7] and about 100 independent establishments, nearly half of which were engaged in teaching English as a foreign language.

Non-vocational 'Adult Education' was provided by universities, voluntary bodies, notably the Workers Educational Association (WEA), and the LEAs. Statistics are unreliable, because many studies in LEA colleges can be pursued for either vocational or non-vocational aims, and because of the great disparity in university and WEA courses between the number of registered and of 'effective' students – i.e. those who follow right through a course. The number of Adult Education students has been greatly increased since 1971 by the Open University, which is described in Chapter 10.

Primary and Secondary Education

(A) PREMISES

Premises for Primary and Secondary schools are provided by:

1. *Local Education Authorities.* These schools are called *County* schools. They constitute a large and growing majority of the total number provided. In January 1975 there were about 19,000 County schools or departments out of a total (excluding Nursery and Special schools) of about 28,000 maintained by LEAs.

2. *Non-statutory bodies.* There were in 1975 about 9,000 maintained schools or departments provided by non-statutory bodies, the vast majority of whom have

religious affiliations; about 6,000 schools belonged to bodies attached to the Church of England and about 2,600 to the Roman Catholic Church. The schools provided by non-statutory bodies are called *Voluntary* schools. They fall into three categories:

(a) Voluntary Controlled Schools

The premises of these schools remain the property of the providing body, but the LEA meets all the expenses, both recurrent and capital. In 1975 there were about 3,800 Voluntary Controlled schools, all except about 225 provided by bodies associated with the Church of England. The Roman Catholic Church will not accept controlled status.

(b) Voluntary Aided Schools

For these the LEA meets all the running costs, but the providing body has to meet part of the capital cost of any improvement or enlargement of the premises. The providing body is also responsible for the maintenance of the exterior of the fabric. Under the 1944 Act the Government could make a grant in aid of capital expenditure of up to 50 per cent of the total cost. This limit has been progressively raised; by 1975 it was 85 per cent. There were then just over 5,000 Voluntary Aided schools, nearly half of them Roman Catholic schools.

(c) Special Agreement Schools

This is a small group arising out of an agreement made under the Education Act 1936, whereby LEAs were empowered to make grants covering 50 to 75 per cent of the cost of building Voluntary Senior Elementary schools under the 'Hadow' reorganization. By the outbreak of the 1939–45 war few of the 509 agreements made had been carried out, and the Education Act, 1944 allowed for their revival.

In 1975 there were about 130 Special Agreement schools, over three-quarters of them Roman Catholic schools.

(B) RELIGIOUS INSTRUCTION AND WORSHIP

The categories of Voluntary Controlled and Voluntary Aided schools are the result of an agreement made between the State and the religious denominations concerned and embodied in the Education Act 1944. The conditions of financial aid from the State to Voluntary schools are determined by the degree of freedom in respect of denominational religious instruction and worship accorded to a school.

The 1944 Act laid down (for the first time) that in all maintained Primary and Secondary schools each school day must, wherever practicable, commence with an act of corporate worship, and that regular and systematic religious instruction must be given. In County schools the worship must be undenominational in character, and the instruction in accordance with an Agreed Syllabus drawn up, for each LEA area, by a statutory committee which is representative of the

LEA, the teachers' professional associations and the religious denominations concerned in that area. In Voluntary Controlled schools the same conditions obtain, except that the schools have the right to give denominational religious instruction during not more than two school periods each week to children whose parents desire them to receive it. In Voluntary Aided schools the managers or governors have complete control of the religious education given. This is also the case in Special Agreement schools.

(C) SCHOOL GOVERNMENT

In 1976 every County or Voluntary Primary school had by law to have a Board of Managers, of not fewer than six persons, every County or Voluntary Secondary school a Board of Governors, of such number as the LEA (for County schools) or the Secretary of State (for Voluntary schools) should determine. For Voluntary Aided and Special Agreement schools two-thirds of the managers or governors had to be 'foundation' members, that is, representative of the body which provides the school, and one-third representative of the LEA. For Voluntary Controlled schools these proportions were reversed. For County schools all the managers or governors were appointed by the LEA. Two or more schools might be grouped under a single Board of Managers or Governors, and this was frequently done, especially with County schools.

The instrument of management or government for a County school was made by the LEA, for a Voluntary school by the Secretary of State.

In January 1975 the Secretary of State, Mr Reg Prentice, announced that the Government had decided to make "a fundamental examination of the government and management of schools". In April he announced that, in conjunction with the Secretary of State for Wales, he had appointed a Committee of Enquiry, under the chairmanship of Mr Tom Taylor. This committee was still pursuing its investigations at the end of 1976.

(D) THE PRIMARY STAGE

The Primary stage of education, which may be preceded by Nursery education (two to five), was in 1976 usually divided into Infant education (5 to 7+) and Junior education (7+ to 11+). (There were only about 1,150 Middle schools, of which less than half were 'deemed Primary'.) Where Middle schools exist, the school preceding them is usually called the 'First' school – as recommended in the 'Plowden' Report on *Children and their Primary Schools*.

Nursery education is voluntary. It is given in Nursery schools, which may admit pupils from the age of two, and in Nursery classes attached to Primary schools, which may admit children from the age of three. In 1976 there were about 45,000 children spending the whole day and over 100,000 part of the day in maintained Nursery schools and classes. All Nursery schools and classes are co-educational. The maximum number of children allowed by Regulations in a

Water play in a nursery school

nursery class is thirty. Every maintained or aided Nursery school must be in the charge of a qualified teacher.

No formal lessons are given in Nursery schools and classes. The rooms are furnished as well-equipped nurseries, in which the children learn, under the skilled supervision of the teacher, to live and play and work happily together. Training in good personal and social habits is regarded as extremely important, and great attention is paid to physical development.

For Infant education children may be taught either in separate schools, or departments, or in a combined Infant and Junior school. In 1976 there were about twice as many combined as separate schools. When Primary schools are large there is usually an independent head teacher for each department, but in small schools the two departments are under one head.

In 1976 all the Infant and First schools were co-educational. In the first year, the 'reception' class as it is called, the children are as a rule occupied with activities very similar to those in a Nursery school or class. There will be, however, in the classroom various kinds of material from which children may begin to acquire the rudiments of reading and number, and to learn to draw and paint, to measure and to weigh, to buy and sell, and to use cutting and other tools. Music, dance, and rhythmic movement play important parts. Teaching methods with older infants vary considerably. Some teachers introduce more formal instruction; others continue to rely largely upon individual and group activities. An increasing number of teachers is using the technique of 'Family', or 'Vertical', grouping; that is, grouping together children over an age-range of two years or more. In some schools the children's activities will be supervised by teachers working in teams. This is most frequently the case when the premises are 'Open Plan', that is, containing no walled-in classrooms, but only different-sized spaces designed and equipped for different kinds of activities.

In Primary schools organized on the Infant-Junior pattern the children leave the Infant department and enter the Junior between the ages of seven and eight, sometimes moving into another school, sometimes merely transferring to another part of the same building. A few Junior schools are single-sex, but the great majority are co-educational.

More class teaching takes place in the Junior than in the Infants' school, though in many schools this is largely confined, at any rate during the earlier years, to the basic subjects of English and arithmetic (or mathematics), much of the work in history, geography, scripture, nature study, art, and crafts being done in individual or group projects. Music, chiefly choral, but often including instrumental work, is often a delightful mixture of the formal and informal. Extensive experiments have taken place since 1944 in Primary school methodology. Notable results have included entirely new approaches to the teaching and learning of mathematics and science, and the introduction of French as a regular item in the Junior school curriculum. (The wisdom of the last was in 1974 queried in a report published by the National Foundation for Educational Research.)

Some Junior schools with more than one class in each year were in 1976 still 'streaming' their pupils into classes of children as nearly equal in ability as possible, but there has been for years a growing movement in favour of 'unstreamed', or 'mixed ability', classes. Streaming is done partly to ease the teacher's task, partly to suit the content and pace of the instruction to the children's varied abilities, and partly to give the abler children a better chance in any selection tests by which they may be allocated to suitable forms of secondary education.

Content and methods in Middle schools depend largely upon whether a school has been deemed Primary or Secondary. As Middle schools of either type constitute a new departure in English education, both offer the widest scope for experiment, especially in purpose-built premises.

(E) SELECTION FOR SECONDARY EDUCATION

Until 1964 all children in maintained schools had by law to be transferred from primary to secondary education between the ages of ten and a half and twelve. To ensure that, so far as could be predicted, they would receive appropriate secondary education, they were during their last year in Primary school subjected to a battery of tests, popularly known as the 'Eleven-plus exam' (described in Chapter 5). As Comprehensive schools became more numerous the incidence of the Eleven-plus decreased, but owing to fluctuations of governmental policy about comprehensivization, different LEA attitudes towards selection for secondary education, and widespread demand from parents for the retention of Grammar schools, it had not entirely disappeared by the end of 1976.

(F) SECONDARY EDUCATION

For many years after the passing of the 1944 Act there was a mounting tide of opposition to the 'Eleven-plus' and the consequential segregation of children in different types of schools attracting different degrees of public esteem. By the late 1950s, though secondary education in maintained schools was still largely organized on the tripartite basis of Grammar, Technical, and Modern schools, the originally sharp dividing lines between these types had in many places become somewhat blurred, and a number of Comprehensive schools had been set up.

In 1965 a Labour Party Secretary of State, Mr Anthony Crosland, in Circular 10/65 'requested' all LEAs to submit plans for reorganizing their Secondary schools on Comprehensive lines. By 1970 about 130 LEAs, out of the then total of 164, had had their plans approved; and there were about 1,200 Comprehensive schools – nearly one-third of the total number of maintained Secondary schools. But in July of that year a Conservative Secretary of State, Mrs Margaret Thatcher, withdrew Circular 10/65, and substituted Circular 10/70, in which she offered LEAs the freedom to plan as they wished. She did not, however, prevent building schemes already started from going ahead, and by 1973 the number of Comprehensive schools had risen to over 1,800. In 1974 the Labour Party returned to power, and at once re-affirmed its 1965 policy. By January 1976 there were about 3,300 Comprehensive schools, housing about 55 per cent of the pupils in maintained Secondary schools.

The Grammar school (or course), which caters for (on average) the 20 per cent most intellectually able children, provides an academic curriculum leading to the examinations for the General Certificate of Education (GCE), and to university or other higher education. The Technical Secondary school provides curricula biased towards some employment or group of employments, the most common being engineering for boys and commercial subjects for girls. The number of Technical Secondary schools, never much above 300, was decreasing long before Comprehensive reorganization began. The Secondary Modern school, product of the 1944 Act, was previously the senior part of the Elementary school. By definition the school for children below the topmost levels of intellectual ability, it catered for some 70 per cent of the secondary school population and therefore for a very wide range of ability. During the 1950s and 1960s it developed into various different types of school, ranging from some almost as academic as the Grammar school, through others providing, like the Technical Secondary school, vocationally biased courses, to those which spent much time on the basic studies of English and mathematics and the practice of various handicrafts. Many schools provided, for their more intellectually able pupils, academic courses leading to GCE. In 1965 a new external examination, for the Certificate of Secondary Education (CSE), was introduced: it was intended particularly to meet the needs of the Secondary Modern school.

The various developments in secondary education led to a number of amalgamations of schools. Many resulted in 'Bilateral' schools, that is, schools providing two of the three main types of secondary education. Most Bilaterals were Grammar-Modern, but there were also some Grammar-Technical and a few Technical-Modern. From 1947 onwards there were also experiments with Comprehensive schools, that is, schools

. . . intended to cater for all the secondary education of all the children in a given area, without an organization in three sides.[8]

During the following fifteen years the number of Comprehensive schools grew slowly, mainly in the areas of a few LEAs, notably Anglesey, Coventry, and London. Until 1957 all the schools covered the whole period of secondary education (eleven to eighteen-plus) in one establishment. In 1957 Leicestershire began to experiment with a 'two-tier' plan, under which all children transferred at eleven-plus (or thereabouts) from Primary school to 'High School', and at fourteen could opt either to remain in the High School until the end of 'compulsory school age' (i.e. fifteen-plus), or to transfer to a 'Grammar school' (with a wider curriculum than the normal Grammar school), a condition being that they would remain there at least two years. This 'Leicestershire Plan' was included among the six types of Comprehensive organization specified in Circular 10/65. Since then schools of all these types have been established, but up to the time of writing (March 1977) the 'all-through' (11–18) has remained the most popular.

Outside the statutory system there were in 1976 about 2,300 independent schools in England and Wales, ranging in character from small kindergartens to such famous 'public' schools as Eton and Harrow. Of these schools over half had, at their own request, been specially inspected by HMI, and were 'Recognized as Efficient' by the DES.

No independent school may receive any grants from public funds; but LEAs may make agreements with independent schools whereby the schools accept pupils whose tuition fees are paid, in whole or in part, by the authority.

From 30 September 1957 all independent schools have had to be registered with the DES in accordance with the terms of Part III of the Education Act 1944, which came into operation on that day. It is a legal offence to open or conduct an unregistered school, and the Act gives the Secretary of State powers to close (subject to appeal) schools inefficiently or improperly conducted or inadequately housed.

Education of Handicapped Children

Varied provision is made for the education of children handicapped by physical or mental defect. Much extension and improvement were made possible by the Education Act 1944, which expanded the previous narrow limits of ascertainment and 'special educational treatment' to cover all children suffering 'from any disability of mind or body', and required the Minister to define the categories of disability, so that children might receive special educational treatment appropriate to their particular needs. These are the categories.[9]

Blind	Partially sighted
Deaf	Partially hearing
Educationally subnormal	Maladjusted
Epileptic	Physically handicapped
Delicate	Aphasic (Speech Defects)

Special educational treatment for handicapped children is provided in special classes in ordinary Primary and Secondary schools, in day and boarding 'Special' schools, in hospital Special schools, and pupils' homes. National policy is to keep handicapped children in ordinary schools whenever this can be done without detriment to themselves or their schoolfellows. If the disability requires a Special school, a day-school is used if practicable, boarding education being reserved for cases of serious handicap.

In 1975 LEAs were maintaining about 1,500 Special schools, containing altogether about 120,000 children; and Voluntary Bodies receiving direct grants from the DES were maintaining about 110 schools accommodating about 9,000 children. Of the 1,600 Special schools rather more than one-third were day-schools containing over two-thirds of the children. By far the largest group of handicapped children is the educationally subnormal (ESN); in 1975 it accounted for half the number of Special schools, and more than half the children. Though the number of ESN schools has increased since 1944 to more than double the number of all other Special schools, there has always been a waiting list, often of ten to twelve thousand children.

The Education (Handicapped Children) Act 1970 transferred, from 1 April 1971, responsibility for the education of severely subnormal (ESN/S) children from the DHSS to the DES. About 30,000 children were involved.

Welfare Services

For children between the ages of two and eighteen in attendance at maintained schools there are available:

1 *Child Health Services*. These provide, free of charge to parents, a comprehensive range of integrated health services for children.
2 *A School Meals Service*. This provides daily cooked midday meals, and other refreshments where needed, at a relatively small cost. The charge is remitted for children of necessitous parents.
3 *A School Milk Service*. For over twenty years after the 1939–45 war this provided free milk to all children in maintained schools; but in 1968 Secondary school children were excluded, and in 1971 the supply was restricted to children under eight in ordinary schools, children in Special schools, and other children for whom milk had been recommended by a doctor.
4 *Clothing and Cleanliness Services*
5 *A Transport Service*
6 *A Careers Service*

Child Health Services

The Education Act 1944 made it the duty of the L E A to provide free medical and dental inspection and treatment for all pupils in maintained schools and students in county colleges, and gave it the power to provide such inspection and treatment for pupils in other maintained establishments, and, by arrangement with proprietors, for pupils in independent schools or colleges.

From 1 April 1945, when Part Two of the 1944 Act came into operation, until 31 March 1974 LEAs maintained for these purposes a School Health Service, staffed by medical and dental officers, psychiatrists, psychologists, nurses, dental attendants, and other staff. They carried out every year some millions of routine inspections, and provided, or arranged for, a vast amount of medical and dental treatment, including hospital treatment. The School Health Service, while co-operating with the National Health Service, functioned as an autonomous body, administered in each LEA area by a Principal School Medical Officer and a Principal School Dental Officer, both of whom the LEA had by law to appoint.

Under the National Health Service Reorganisation Act 1973, which came into operation on 1 April 1974, the School Health Service was combined with the health services for pre-school children, the health services for children provided by general medical and dental practitioners, and the hospital and specialist services, to provide a comprehensive range of integrated health services for children. Responsibility for this was vested in Area Health Authorities (AHAs) working under the control and direction of the Secretary of State for Health and Social Security. The areas of the AHAs are (except in the Greater London area) identical with those of the new LEAs created by the Local Government Act 1972.

It remains the duty of the LEA to ascertain children in need of special educational treatment, and to provide the nurses, dentists, speech therapists, and other health staff required in Special schools. The LEA has also to make available accommodation for the medical inspection of school children. The LEA's agreement must be secured when chief AHA officers are appointed, and one of these, the specialist in community medicine (child health), while responsible to the AHA, is directly accountable to the LEA for the advice he gives to it and to the teachers in its employ, and for ensuring that medical and other health service staff are available to enable the LEA to perform its duty in respect of handicapped children.

Milk and Meals Services

It is the duty of the LEA to provide "milk, meals and other refreshment for pupils at schools . . . maintained by them". The daily milk ration is ordinarily one-third of a pint, but more may be given on medical advice. School milk has remained free. School meals have never been free, though originally they were intended to be. The price of meals has recurrently been increased, to make it approximately equal to the cost of the food. By 1970 almost all maintained schools had facilities for providing meals. Independent schools can arrange with LEAs to participate in the Milk and Meals Services, a condition being that the LEA shall not incur a greater expenditure *per capita* than it does in supplying its own schools.

Clothing and Cleanliness Services

LEAs have power to supply a child with clothing if he appears to be "unable by reason of the inadequacy of his clothing to take full advantage of the education provided at the school". They may supply any children in their schools with clothing for physical education. They can require parents to cleanse medically dirty children, and failing parental co-operation can do the cleansing themselves.

Transport for School Children

If the nearest appropriate school is three miles or more from a child's home, the LEA must by law provide transport to and from school for that child; for children under the age of eight the limit is two miles. LEAs in general pay the children's fares by public transport or hire buses from public or private transport companies. They do not usually run their own fleets of buses, except for the conveyance of physically handicapped children.

Boarding Accommodation

LEAs have power to arrange boarding accommodation, "either in boarding schools or otherwise", for children whom they, and the parents, deem it to be advisable.

Careers Service

From 1948 to 1974 there was a Youth Employment Service (YES), responsible to the Minister of Labour (later, Employment and Productivity), but operated in most areas by the LEAs. Under the Employment and Training Act 1973 it became the responsibility of the LEA to provide a Careers Service to persons of any age who were attending maintained schools or colleges.

Help from Outside Bodies

The number of outside bodies aiding schools is legion. Public libraries, art galleries and museums co-operate largely. Local authorities arrange visits to public services; industrial and other firms to their works and offices. Numerous voluntary bodies give widely various aid. A very large proportion of schools use the School Broadcasting Service (sound radio) provided by the British Broadcasting Corporation (BBC). This offers an organized programme of lessons in many school subjects, and for all age ranges. In 1957 both the BBC and Associated-Rediffusion Ltd., a member of the Independent Television Association (ITA), began providing school television services. By 1970 some LEAs, universities, colleges and schools were making use of closed-circuit television.

All recently built and many other schools are equipped for film projection. Films suitable for schools are available from the National Committee for Audio-Visual Aids in Education (NCAVAE), a body largely financed by the LEAs, from various film-making organizations, and from many governmental and industrial and commercial undertakings which produce them for publicity purposes. Film strips, available from the same sources, are also used extensively by the schools. Many LEAs maintain museum services for loaning collections of exhibits to schools, and the Victoria and Albert Museum, London, operates a national scheme for the loan of reproductions of famous pictures. The National Council for Educational Technology (NCET) produces materials in several media.

Many schools have active Parent-Teacher or Parents' Associations. Many schools organize periodical Open Days, on which parents, relatives, and friends of the pupils are invited to view exhibits of school work and activities. Some LEAs organize Education Days, or Weeks, when all the schools are open to the public, and exhibitions and demonstrations are supplemented by lectures on educational topics.

Further Education

Further Education, as defined in the Education Act 1944, includes all kinds of educational studies and activities, formal and informal, except full-time secondary education and university education, for persons of any age beyond school-leaving age. It covers practically every field of human knowledge and skill, and is provided at every level from that of a pupil who has just left a Secondary school at the age of 16, to post-graduate study and research.

There are three broad categories of Further Education: vocational studies, non-vocational studies, and social and recreative activities. Engaged on vocational studies are full-time, 'sandwich',[10] part-time day, and evening students. Non-vocational studies, and social and recreative activities, are largely evening pursuits.

The great bulk of vocational education is provided by the LEAs, in Colleges of Further Education, which offer a wide variety of mainly non-advanced courses, Colleges of Agriculture and/or Horticulture, of Art and Design, Technology, and other specialisms, offering both non-advanced and advanced courses, and Polytechnics and Colleges and Institutes of Higher Education, which offer only advanced courses.

The field of Further Education has since the late 1950s been undergoing almost continuous reorganization. This began (on a large scale) in 1956 with a rationalization of technical education which grouped the technical colleges on four levels according to the standard of the work they undertook. At the top, ten large technical colleges were designated Colleges of Advanced Technology (CATs), and devoted exclusively to advanced studies. The second group consisted of twenty-five 'Regional' colleges, also occupied largely with advanced studies. Group three was made up of 'Area' colleges – one or more to an LEA area – whose principal function was to provide courses leading from introductory to advanced studies. The most elementary work was done by 'Local', or 'District', colleges, which formed the largest group.

In 1966-7, in accordance with recommendations made by the Robbins committee, the CATs were made universities (or in two cases colleges of universities),[11] and a new top level institution of higher education was created: the Polytechnic. Between 1969 and 1973 thirty Polytechnics were formed, mainly by amalgamating two or more existing colleges, including the Regional colleges.

In the early 1960s the courses and examinations of the Art colleges were reorganized. The Minister of Education ceased to be responsible for these, and the two awards he had been making, the Intermediate Certificate in Art and Crafts, and the National Diploma in Design (NDD), were replaced by a Diploma in Art and Design (Dip AD), which was rated the equivalent of a first degree. The Dip AD courses did not, however, prove wholly satisfactory. In 1974 the National Council for Diplomas in Art and Design (NCDAD) was merged with the Council for National Academic Awards (CNAA).

In 1967 the Secretary of State asked the National Advisory Council on Education for Industry and Commerce (NACEIC) to review the provision of courses suitable for technicians at all levels and comparable grades in non-technical occupations. In 1969 the 'Haslegrave' committee[12] appointed by the NACEIC recommended that the Secretary of State should establish a Technician Education Council (TEC) and a Business Education Council (BEC) to plan, coordinate, and administer national technician and business examinations and qualifications, and introduce a unified pattern of courses that would ultimately replace the existing pattern of National Certificates and Diplomas and the City and Guilds of London Institute awards. The TEC was set up in 1973 and the BEC in 1974.

In December 1972 the Government outlined in a White Paper entitled *Education: A Framework for Expansion*,[13] its projected development plan for the years up to 1981. This covered the entire field of public education, but was largely concerned with higher education, including the training of teachers, about which a committee appointed by the Secretary of State for Education and Science, the 'James' committee,[14] had reported twelve months previously. The White Paper proposed that most Colleges of Education should cease to be devoted exclusively to the training of teachers, and should provide also other types of courses, either as independent institutions, or merged with Polytechnics or Colleges of Further Education. To enable students to defer decision about their careers, it endorsed the Diploma in Higher Education (Dip HE) recommended by the James Committee, obtainable through a two-year full-time course, and serving either as a terminal qualification, or as leading to a degree or comparable qualification.

Discussions about the futures of the individual Colleges of Education began in 1973.[15] They were continually hampered by successively decreasing projections of the number of teachers that would be required in 1981 – and consequently of the number to be trained. Although by the end of 1976 the destinies of over 100 of the colleges appeared to have been determined, mainly by mergers, the continued existence of many others was still at risk.

Liberal studies for adults are called 'Adult Education'. While the LEAs provide considerable facilities for Adult Education, much of this is done by voluntary organizations, usually with grant-aid from either the DES or the LEAs. A number of institutions have the status of 'Responsible Bodies'; most of these are either Extra-Mural Departments of Universities or WEA districts. An interesting development since the Second World War has been the establishment, by LEAs and/or voluntary bodies, of over thirty residential Colleges of Adult Education providing short courses ranging in duration from a week-end to a few weeks. There are five older-established residential Colleges of Adult Education providing courses of one year or more.[16] All receive direct grants from the DES.

Facilities for social and recreative activities are provided by LEAs, voluntary youth organizations, and numerous other voluntary bodies, national and local. The range is from physical education and outdoor games to discussion groups, and includes all sorts of hobbies, handicrafts and domestic occupations.

University Education

There were in 1976 thirty-five Universities in England (including the 'Open' University), and one in Wales. The Universities of Oxford and Cambridge are over 750 years old. London and Durham were founded in the early part of the nineteenth century, Manchester and Wales towards its close; the others are twentieth century foundations.

In 1975 the Universities of England and Wales (excluding the Open University) contained over 220,000 full-time students (nearly 70 per cent men), of whom approximately four-fifths were reading for a first degree; the others (a small minority excepted) were doing post-graduate work or research. About 23 per cent studied pure science, 12 per cent engineering, 8 per cent medicine, dentistry and health, and 25 per cent social, administrative and business studies.

First degrees fall broadly into two categories: (1) 'General', 'Ordinary', or 'Pass', and (2) 'Honours', or 'Special'. General degrees involve study of three or four subjects, and the course normally takes three years. Honours degrees involve specialization in one subject or one or two allied subjects; most of the courses are of three years' duration, but some extend over four.

In 1975 about 45 per cent of students lived in colleges, halls of residence, or other university accommodation, about 37 per cent in lodgings or flats, and under 20 per cent in their own homes. The proportion of students living in colleges and halls of residence ranged from over 80 per cent at the University of Keele to less than a quarter at some of the newest Universities. Several Universities were providing flats and other self-service accommodation for students.

Over 90 per cent of the students received financial assistance towards payment of tuition fees and cost of maintenance. Most of this assistance came from public funds. The chief sources of aid were:

(*a*) Open scholarships, exhibitions and other awards made by the Universities, especially Oxford and Cambridge.

(*b*) Awards made each year by LEAs. This was by far the largest source, because the Education Act 1962 imposed upon the LEAs a statutory duty to make awards to all suitably qualified students.

(*c*) State Studentships awarded annually by the DES to post-graduate students in the Humanities.

(*d*) Awards made by the five Research Councils (Agricultural, Medical, Natural Environment, Science, and Social Science) to post-graduate students.

(*e*) Scholarships offered, almost exclusively to students of science or technology, by various industrial undertakings and by HM Forces.

All grants for first degree or comparable courses made by the DES and the LEAs were on a sliding scale related to the income of the student's parents, or the student himself if of independent status. The scales are revised periodically. Awards made by industrial concerns and HM Forces are not usually subject to a means test, and they ordinarily carry grants large enough to cover the cost of tuition fees and maintenance.

Training of Teachers

Following recommendations made in the McNair Report, between 1947 and 1955 all the Universities[17] except Cambridge undertook responsibility for the education and training of prospective teachers, and for awarding the Teacher's Certificate. The co-ordination and supervision of the courses and examinations in the training colleges in each University's area was performed, on behalf of the University, by an Area Training Organisation (ATO) representative of the University, the training colleges, the LEAs, and the teachers. Each ATO was serviced by an Institute of Education[18] provided, maintained, and staffed by the university. [19] The Vice-Chancellor of the University was *ex-officio* chairman of the governing body of the ATO, and most of the directors of the Institutes were accorded the rank of professor.

There were three main types of teacher-training establishments: University Departments of Education (UDEs), Colleges of Education (up to 1963 called Training Colleges), and Art Training Centres (ATCs). From 1967 onwards there were also training departments in a few Polytechnics. UDEs accepted only graduates, whom they gave one academic year of professional training. ATCs accepted only men and women professionally trained as artists and/or craftsmen; these also received one year of training for teaching. Colleges of Education were by far the most numerous; there were about 160, as compared with about 25 UDEs and a dozen ATCs.[20] But there were three types of training colleges: 'general', about 135 in number, which prepared teachers for ordinary class work, mostly in Primary schools; 'specialist', which trained women to teach domestic science (about fifteen colleges), or physical education (seven colleges); and 'technical', which trained men and women for work in Further Education. For most of the period there were only three Colleges of Education (Technical), but in 1961 a fourth was added. Before 1960 the general colleges gave a two-year course, of concurrent personal education and professional training; in September 1960 their course was lengthened to three years. The Colleges of Education (Technical) accepted men and women aged 25 or more (or younger if they were graduates), required of them vocational as well as academic qualifications, and offered them a one-year pre-service course, and courses of various lengths if they were serving teachers.

The UDEs were provided and maintained by their Universities. Four of the ATCs were in Universities,[21] the others in Colleges of Art (some of which were later absorbed into Polytechnics). Of the 160 or so Colleges of Education about

110 were provided by LEAs, and about 50 by voluntary bodies, most of which were associated with religious denominations. About half were Church of England, one-third (in 1975) Roman Catholic.

This system was in process of dissolution in 1976, but the final shape of the system which would replace it was far from settled. Such information as was available at the time of writing (March 1977) is given in Chapter 11.

Policy Making

In the making of national policy for education the Secretary of State for Education and Science has the final say, subject to the over-riding authority of Parliament. But in the framing of policy the LEAs and the teachers, through their professional associations, play a very important part; they are taken into consultation on most matters of substance, and the initiative in making proposals frequently comes from them.

The principal teachers' associations are:

The National Union of Teachers (NUT), which has members from all branches of the statutory system, from independent schools and Universities. The great bulk of its membership is from the maintained Primary and Secondary schools. It is by far the largest of the associations.

The Joint Four Secondary Associations (Joint Four), comprising:

The Incorporated Association of Headmasters of Secondary Schools (IAHM);
The Association of Headmistresses (HMA);
The Incorporated Association of Assistant Masters in Secondary Schools (IAAM):
The Association of Assistant Mistresses in Secondary Schools (AAM).

The National Association of Head Teachers (NAHT) which is chiefly representative of maintained Primary and Secondary schools.

The National Association of Schoolmasters (NAS), founded to defend specifically male interests, after the introduction of equal pay for men and women (1955–61) extended its range to cover the entire field of public education. In 1975 it amalgamated with *The Union of Women Teachers* (UWT), originally founded to fight for equal pay; the two became the NAS/UWT.

The Headmasters' Conference (HMC). Membership is confined to Heads of Public schools.

The National Association of Teachers in Further and Higher Education (NATFHE), formed January 1976 by amalgamating *The Association of Teachers in Technical Institutions* (ATTI) and *The Association of Teachers in Colleges and Departments of Education* (ATCDE).

The Association of University Teachers (AUT).

There are also many subject associations, such as the Mathematical Association, the Modern Languages Association, the Association for Science Education and the Physical Education Association.

Most of these associations publish regular periodicals. The most widely known is *The Teacher* (formerly *The Schoolmaster*), the official journal of the NUT. It is published weekly.

The local authority associations concerned with education are:

The Council of Local Education Authorities (CLEA), a body appointed jointly by *The Association of Metropolitan Authorities* (AMA) and *The Association of County Councils* (ACC).

The Association of Education Committees (AEC) was formerly representative of almost all the education committees of local authorities in England and Wales, but after the 1974 reorganization only of a smaller number. It closed down in March 1977. The weekly paper *Education* was its official journal.

Among other bodies which concern themselves actively with educational matters are:

The National Union of Students (NUS). Membership of this is open to students in Universities and colleges of higher education.
The Workers' Educational Association (WEA).
The Confederation of British Industries (CBI).
The Trades Union Congress (TUC).
The British Council of Churches.

References

1 The Transfer of Functions (Wales) Order 1970.
2 The Secretary of State for Education and Science Order 1964.
3 Education Act 1944, First Schedule, Part II (1).
4 So called from the name of the first chairman, Viscount Burnham.
5 *Direct Grant Grammar Schools (Cessation of Grant) Regulations 1975* (SI 1975 No. 1198).
6 The Polytechnics in the ILEA area are grant-aided.
7 The College of Air Training, the School of Automotive Studies, the National College of Agricultural Engineering, and the National Leathersellers College.
8 Circular 144, *Organisation of Secondary Education*, dated 16 June, 1947.
9 *The Handicapped Pupils and Special Schools Regulations 1959,* (SI 1959, No. 365).
10 'Sandwich' courses alternate periods of some length in college and relevant employment.
11 Chelsea Polytechnic and Cardiff College of Technology.
12 The chairman was Dr H. L. Haslegrave, the recently retired first Vice-Chancellor of Loughborough University.
13 Cmnd. 5174. HMSO, 1972.
14 *Teacher Education and Training*. HMSO, 1972.

15 See Cireular 7/73, *Development of Higher Education in the non-University Sector*, dated 26 March 1973.

16 Ruskin College, Oxford; Plater (formerly the Catholic Workers) College, Oxford; Fircroft College, Birmingham; Hillcroft College, Surbiton; Co-operative College, Loughborough; Coleg Harlech, North Wales. Fircroft was closed in 1975 by an internal dispute.

17 The word 'universities' here includes the five University Colleges of Hull, Leicester, Nottingham, Southampton, and the South-West (Exeter). All these became Universities between 1948 and 1957.

18 The Universities of Manchester and Wales established Schools of Education.

19 The Cambridge Institute of Education was provided and maintained by the Minister (later Secretary of State) of Education. The University of Cambridge was represented on its governing body.

20 The numbers in all three categories varied slightly over the years.

21 London, which had two: one in the Institute of Education and one in Goldsmiths' College; Newcastle, and Reading.

Further Reading

ALEXANDER, SIR WILLIAM (now Lord), *Education in England*. Newnes Educational, 2nd edition, 1964.

BARON, G., *Society, Schools and Progress in England*. Pergamon, 1965.

BURGESS, TYRELL, *A Guide to English Schools*. Penguin, 3rd edition, 1972.

PARRY, J. P., *The Provision of Education in England and Wales*. Allen & Unwin, 1971.

PETERS, A. J., *British Further Education*. Pergamon, 1967.

Official

Ministry of Education and, from 1964, DES Annual Reports. Statistics were included in these up to and including 1960; since then, *Statistics of Education* have been published separately, in several volumes each year.

The Health of the School Child. Report of the Chief Medical Officer, usually published every two years.

Reports on Education. Broadsheets on a wide variety of topics. Published somewhat irregularly, but roughly at monthly intervals. Obtainable gratis from the DES.

Trends in Education. Quarterly, DES.

Dialogue. Termly, Schools Council.

Commonwealth Universities Year Book. Association of Commonwealth Universities (ACU).

CHAPTER 3 | # Control and Direction

In writing about control of education in England and Wales, it is necessary to say at the outset that there can be all the difference in the world between the letter of the law and the way in which this is interpreted in practice. On paper, for example, Section 1 of the Education Act 1944 accords to the Minister of Education[1] virtually dictatorial powers over the LEAs, who are put "under his control and direction". No Minister has yet used those powers dictatorially – though one or two have come near to it – and there would be a first-class political crisis if this happened. Consultation and negotiation are the means that he or she is expected to employ, and in fact does employ. Moreover, in practice, well understood and accepted powers of control and direction are vested in bodies and individuals at all levels in the educational system. In some cases these powers have little or no sanction in law. Take, for example, the case of the Primary school head teacher, whose power within his school is not only substantial but is acknowledged to be so. But the 1944 Act offers no definition of his duties, powers, or responsibilities, though it does (in Section 17(3)(b)) in the case of the Secondary school head. Alongside this wide distribution of powers – which has developed almost entirely during the present century – there has grown up also an intricate network of checks designed to prevent the undue or irresponsible use of power by any organization or individual; and this, again, is only in part sanctioned by law. But too much must not be made of checks and balances; what really makes the English educational system 'tick' is the fact that the various parties who have to work it – central and local administrators, teachers, and voluntary bodies – regard and treat each other as partners. They quarrel at times – what partners do not? – and the 'locals' are always alert (not without reason) to ensure that the Centre does not become too much the dominant partner; but both the idea and the practice of partnership remain constant.

All this must be borne in mind as one examines the hierarchy of control and direction. Ultimate control rests with Parliament (as representative of the electorate), which enacts the law relating to education, and by various means assures itself that it is being observed. The Secretary of State for Education and Science (for brevity's sake ordinarily referred to in these pages as simply the Secretary of State), to whom Parliament delegates the responsibility for 'control and direction' of the statutory system, has to make an annual report to Parliament on the state of the system,[2] and his presentation of this report is invariably the occasion for a full-length debate in the House of Commons. In addition, any member of either House of Parliament may at any time request a debate on a specified educational topic. All Regulations (which have the force of law) which the Secretary of State proposes to make, as required or permitted by the Education Acts, must be "laid before Parliament",[3] that is, be available in the House for scrutiny by Members, for a period of forty Parliamentary days before they can be put into operation; during this period any Member has the right to ask Parliament to annul them. And any Member of the House of Commons may on any Parliamentary day ask the Secretary of State in the House a question (or more than one) about any educational matter within his jurisdiction.[4] It is by this last means that Parliament keeps itself most constantly informed. Any MP may also seek information privately from the Secretary of State, or draw his attention to alleged defects or injustice.

By a tradition that has become firmly established during the present century Parliament does not prescribe in legislation what shall be taught in schools and colleges. A striking exception to this otherwise sacrosanct tradition was, however, made in 1944, when for the first time in the history of the statutory system religious instruction and worship were made compulsory in all maintained schools.[5] Parliament does not prescribe any text or other books, or give any directions about teaching methods; and MPs who ask questions about such matters are usually told firmly by the Secretary of State that they are the concern of the teacher.

Secretary of State for Education and Science

By the Education Act 1944 personal responsibility to Parliament for the statutory system of public education was vested in a Minister of Education. Twenty years later, on 1 April 1964, all the functions of the Minister of Education for England and Wales, and of the Minister of Science, were by Order in Council transferred to a Secretary of State for Education and Science, who was made responsible not only for the statutory system of education in England and Wales, but also for the Parliamentary grant to the Universities and University Colleges, and to 'Civil Science', that is, scientific research and development devoted to non-military purposes, throughout Great Britain. In 1965 he was also (under the Public Libraries and Museums Act 1964) required to superintend, and promote the improvement of, the Public Library Service. In 1970 his responsibility for Primary and Secondary education in Wales was transferred to the Secretary of State for Wales.

The Secretary of State is assisted in his Parliamentary and Departmental duties by Ministers of State and Parliamentary Under-Secretaries of State. The number of these tends to vary within narrow limits; in 1976 there was one of each. Each had specific fields of responsibility. As the political head of the educational system the Secretary of State must be a Member of Parliament. He is *ex officio* a senior Minister of the Crown, and in recent years has almost invariably had a seat in the Cabinet.

It is important to note that the Secretary of State is held *personally* responsible to Parliament for the proper conduct of the educational system. He is, in the words of the Education Act 1944, a "corporation sole",[6] that is, a corporate body in himself, and as such responsible for everything that is done in his name or by his agents. This is in accordance with the English convention which holds the head of any undertaking responsible for whatever happens within it.

The statutory duty laid upon the Minister of Education by the 1944 Act is a positive one. It is:

to *promote* the education of the people of England and Wales and the *progressive development* of institutions devoted to that purpose, and to *secure the effective execution*, by local authorities *under his control and direction*, of the *national policy* for providing a *varied and comprehensive educational service* in every area.[7]

The words I have italicized can, most of them, be interpreted in very different ways; and so the first, and most important, function of the Secretary of State is to determine how they shall be translated into terms of policy and action. In coming to his decisions he can hardly fail to be largely influenced by the views of the political party to which he belongs; for he will have to secure the agreement to major policy decisions of his colleagues in the Cabinet, and in particular of the Prime Minister, who presumably has the last word in policy making, and of the Chancellor of the Exchequer, who will have to provide the necessary money. In order to place before the Cabinet practicable and (he hopes) acceptable proposals he will previously have had consultations with his professional advisers in the DES, with representatives of the LEAs and of the teachers, and any other bodies concerned. By far the most important, and most difficult, part of the Secretary of State's work is done behind the scenes.

His second function is to be the principal spokesman for public education, both in Parliament and among the general public – for, like every other Minister of the Crown, he is expected to undertake a heavy programme of public engagements, at almost all of which he is expected to make carefully prepared speeches on educational matters. And, thirdly, he is in charge of the DES, and responsible for all the decisions taken there and for the administrative action which consequently follows.

Unlike Ministers of Education in many countries, the Secretary of State does not exercise jurisdiction over all forms of education. Education within the Armed Forces and their auxiliary Services is controlled by the Secretary of State for Defence. 'Community Homes' (formerly called 'Approved schools') for juvenile delinquents and children in care, and Borstal institutions for older delinquents are the concern of the Secretary of State for the Home Department (the 'Home Office').

Nor does the Secretary of State have to undertake a number of functions which are commonly the responsibility of Ministers of Education in other countries. He does not provide, own, or control directly any school, college, or other educational establishment. He does not appoint, employ, pay or dismiss any teachers. He does not prescribe, veto, or censor any books or other printed material, or prescribe or veto any other kinds of equipment and apparatus for use in schools and other educational establishments. He does not prescribe, compile, alter, or veto any curricula, or dictate or prohibit any teaching methods.

The functions of the LEAs will be discussed in detail later, but it is opportune to observe at this point that, in practice, it is often difficult, if not impossible, to determine exactly where the Secretary of State's responsibility ends (except in the general sense that ultimately he is responsible for everything done under the law relating to education), and theirs begins. The lines of demarcation are, in fact, recurrently a source of dispute between central and local authorities. In 1951 a Government committee, in an attempt to produce an agreed formula, suggested that there were six key points at which the Minister must retain control. He must, said the Committee, be able to ensure that:

(*a*) Educational facilities and ancillary services are provided in sufficient quantity and variety.

(*b*) Educational establishments and ancillary services are well managed, equipped, staffed, and maintained.

(*c*) The proper freedom of parents, teachers, and other third parties is secured.

(*d*) The qualifications of teachers and medical officers are such as to satisfy proper requirements to safeguard both their interests and the children's.

(*e*) The fees charged, and awards and allowances made, are such as are necessary and appropriate.

(*f*) The provision of education premises satisfies essential standards.[8]

These proposals were accepted in principle by the Government, the Minister of Education and the representatives of the LEAs, but this did not put an end to the problem. In terms of current practice, the Secretary of State's functions include the following. He has to:

1. Set minimum standards of educational provision.

2. Control the rate, distribution and nature of educational building.

3. Control the supply of teachers, and determine the principles governing the recognition of teachers as Qualified Teachers.

4. Administer a superannuation scheme for teachers.

5. Arrange for the incorporation of estimates of LEAs' expenditure in the general grant made by Parliament to local authorities.

6. Support financially by direct grant a number of institutions of special kinds.

7. Settle disputes between bodies exercising powers within the educational system.

8. Maintain a register of independent schools.

All these functions relate to the educational system; the list does not cover his responsibilities in respect of the Universities and Civil Science.

The Secretary of State, in accordance with the directions of the Education Acts, makes known to the LEAs, and other bodies where these are concerned, his requirements for the organization and administration of the educational system, and the conditions on which grants will be paid from the Exchequer, in bodies of Regulations, officially described as Statutory Rules and Orders (SR & O) or Statutory Instruments (SI). These Regulations, which amplify and make more precise requirements made in brief and general terms in the Education Acts, have the force of law, and consequently are mandatory upon the LEAs and any other bodies to which they refer; failure to comply with them could result in the Secretary of State's refusing to recognize for grant the expenditure affected (where grant is involved), or applying other sanctions – in extreme cases taking over control from the body concerned. Under the Education Act 1944 the Secretary of State is obliged to make some nine bodies of Regulations of the first importance,[9] and has made some twenty others, on matters ranging from the registration of pupils at school to University awards. As need arises amending Regulations are made altering particular points in a main body of Regulations; when several of these have been made, or new legislation requires changes, a revised body of Regulations is made.

The Secretary of State makes known his views on matters of policy and opinion in documents called Circulars. These are not mandatory but advisory or informational, and consequently no LEA, or other body, is legally bound to accept the advice, or adopt any action advocated, in a Circular, though it must be admitted that in some cases Circulars announce Ministerial decisions – for example, about educational building programmes – which leave the local authorities with little opportunity for alternative action. They have, however, the right to dispute points on which they disagree, whereas in the case of a Regulation their only remedy is to persuade the Secretary of State to make a different one.

About matters of routine or detail the Minister issues Administrative Memoranda (AM). These, the most numerous of the Ministerial documents that are made public, may give advice or information, or announce Ministerial decisions. All Regulations, Circulars and Administrative Memoranda are published,[10] and may be purchased by the public.

The content and wording of Regulations are always the subject of discussion – often prolonged – between the Secretary of State, the LEAs, the teachers' associations and any other bodies concerned. So far as is possible Regulations are, by the time they are published, agreed documents; in case, however, of irreconcilable differences of opinion the Secretary of State has the final say. While it is not so vital to obtain unanimous agreement about the terms of Circulars, since these are not mandatory documents, the Secretary of State will, as a rule, consult a wide range of opinion before issuing a Circular on an important matter of national policy. He may send one or more drafts to all the bodies concerned, asking for their comments, and it is possible for weeks, or even months, of consultation and negotiation to take place before an important Circular reaches its final form. It should be made clear, too, that the initiative in making new Regulations or proposing Circulars need not necessarily be taken by the Secretary of State; not infrequently it comes from some other body, or bodies.

According to English tradition, not only is the Secretary of State responsible for all that is done in his name; he is actually supposed to have done himself far more than one person could possibly do. In practice, what he is supposed to have done may have been done by one or other of a great number of people. Only matters deemed really important are put to him for personal decision.

The Ministers and Under-Secretaries who assist the Secretary of State have already been mentioned. He has also at his service in Parliament an MP who acts as his Parliamentary Private Secretary.

The Secretary of State is bound by law to appoint two bodies to give him advice. Section 4(1) of the Education Act 1944 says:

> There shall be two Central Advisory Councils for Education, one for England and the other for Wales and Monmouthshire, and it shall be the duty of those Councils to advise the Minister upon such matters connected with educational theory and practice as they think fit, and upon any questions referred to them by him.

These Councils replaced the Consultative Committee of the Board of Education. Apart from the fact that there are now two – a recognition of the fact that Wales has its own particular problems – a significant change was made in the terms of reference; the Consultative Committee could only advise on matters referred to it by the President of the Board of Education, but the Central Advisory Councils can also take the initiative in proffering advice. In practice they usually work to remits from the Secretary of State.

These are the only advisory bodies which the Secretary of State is statutorily bound to appoint, but they are by no means the only duly constituted bodies which advise him. One of the earliest established was the Secondary School Examinations Council (SSEC), set up in 1917 to advise the President of the Board of Education on policy and arrangements for external examinations. In 1964 its work was taken over by the Schools Council for the Curriculum and Examinations. Since the passing of the 1944 Act there have been created the National Advisory Council on Education for Industry and Commerce (NACEIC, 1948), the National Advisory Council on the Training and Supply of Teachers (NACTST, 1949), which was replaced in 1973 by the Advisory Committee on the Supply and Training of Teachers (ACSTT), the National Advisory Council on Art Education (1959), and the United Kingdom Advisory Council on Education for Management (1960). The Secretary of State may also appoint *ad hoc* committees to advise him on specific problems, and frequently does so.

Schools Council

The Schools Council for the Curriculum and Examinations – called by everyone

'The Schools Council' – was a new departure in English education. Its origin was a 'Curriculum Study Group' set up in the Ministry of Education in 1962 to offer a service of advice and information to the schools, and technical services to the SSEC. Teachers' associations feared that this might lead to Ministry control of school curricula, and persuaded the Minister to appoint a widely representative Working Party to consider whether there was a need for "co-operative machinery to stimulate, organize and co-ordinate fundamental curriculum changes". The Working Party thought there was; and the Schools Council started work in October 1964.

The Council is an independent body representing the entire educational service, including the Universities, but with school teachers forming a majority in its membership. It is financed by the DES and the LEAs in equal proportions. Most of its salaried staff – drawn from the DES, HM Inspectorate, LEA offices, Universities, Colleges, and schools – are seconded on short-term contracts, often of three years. Its functions are "to promote and encourage curriculum study and development without diminishing any of the existing responsibilities of its members, and to sponsor research and enquiry where this is needed to help solve immediate and practical problems". It proved from the start an extremely active body, promoting experiment, research, and development in many sectors of the educational field. Within its first ten years it had embarked upon 160 curriculum projects, ranging from the education of immigrants to technology in schools, and covering most subjects in the school curriculum; had produced numerous research reports and masses of teaching material; and had built up an extensive information service.

The Department of Education and Science

The great bulk of advice and assistance given to the Secretary of State comes, however, from his Department, the Department of Education and Science. This is both his chief source of advice about national policy for education, and his chief means for securing that policy is carried out in practice.

The DES is concerned with the statutory system of education in England and Wales, and with Universities and Civil Science throughout Great Britain. It is staffed by Civil Servants, and has attached to it a corps of HMI. Like all Government Departments, it contains officers of the Administrative Grade, who are occupied with policy making and policy decisions, Professional Officers – lawyers, architects, accountants, and so on – engaged on specialist tasks, and Executive Officers, who carry out the administrative tasks required to translate policy into practice.

The headquarters of the DES are at Elizabeth House, York Road, London SE1 7PH, near Waterloo station. There are nine regional offices in England. The Welsh Education Office has its headquarters in Cardiff, and a small office in Elizabeth House.

The chief administrative officer in the DES is the Permanent Secretary, who is responsible to the Secretary of State for all work done in the Department. Deputy Secretaries oversee schools, HE and FE, Science, Arts and Libraries. Under Secretaries head the Branches into which the DES is divided.

New Branches are not infrequently established, and others altered. The following list must not, therefore, be considered definitive. To keep up to date, consult the DES pamphlet *How DES is Organised*, which is revised periodically. It gives in detail the functions of the Branches.

Schools Branch I Deals with supply and organization of maintained Primary and Secondary schools, Independent schools, nursery education, school transport.

Schools Branch II Liaises with the Schools Council. Covers educational technology, deprivation, race relations, meals and milk, handicapped children, health education, careers.

Teachers Supply and demand, qualifications, salaries.

Pensions Superannuation Acts relating to teachers and some other LEA staff.

Higher and Further Education I Development of non-University Higher Education; training of teachers; government, finance, and administration of Colleges.

Higher and Further Education II Liaison with CNAA; FE building programme, vocational education.

Higher and Further Education III New developments in vocational education, FE provision for the 16 to 19 year olds, careers guidance, industrial training, adult education, Service of Youth.

Higher and Further Education IV University finance, awards to students.

Science Support of civil science research through the research councils (Science, Medical, Agricultural, Natural Environment, Social Science), the Royal Society, Natural History Museum. Responsible for scientific matters in connection with EEC, NATO.

Arts and Libraries Policy on the Arts, including national museums and galleries, and the national libraries.

Finance Financial and accounting policies, estimates, payments, information.

Statistics Statistical and automatic data processing (ADP) services.

Legal Advice to other Branches and the Research Councils, drafting legislation.

External Relations Liaison with educational systems and organizations abroad, teacher and student exchanges, Commonwealth education.

Establishments and Organization Organization, staffing, and accommodation of the DES, including the Victoria and Albert and the Science Museums, which are part of the Department. In this Branch is the Information Division, responsible for relations with the press, radio and TV, and with the general public. The Division includes the DES library.

Architects and Building Building procedures, approval of building projects, statistics of educational building, Building Bulletins, investigation (with HMI and LEAs) of new building trends.

There are also (1) *The Departmental Planning Organization*, a network of committees and groups dealing with medium and long-term planning. Its work is co-ordinated by the Planning Unit, which also administers the DES educational research programme. (2) *The Professional Medical Staff*, which advises all branches, but especially *Schools Branch II* on health services and handicapped pupils. Its head, the *Medical Adviser*, is jointly employed by the DES and the DHSS. (3) *The Assessment of Performance Unit* (APU), set up in 1974 to monitor standards in school subjects.

(4) *Her Majesty's Inspectorate*, whose functions are outlined below.

A Branch is subdivided into divisions, which are in the charge of Assistant Secretaries, and the divisions into sections, in the charge of Principals. All these officers are in the Administrative Grade. New recruits to this grade who are still learning the job, and are not in charge of Sections, are called Assistant Principals. The Welsh Education Office has its own Permanent Secretary, and a similar, but separate, hierarchy of administrative officers.

HM Inspectorate of Schools

As their title suggests, Her Majesty's Inspectors are on a different footing from the other Civil Servants. They are appointed, not by the Secretary of State, but by the Crown – Her Majesty in Council – to whom they are recommended by a selection board which includes the Senior Chief Inspector and a member of the Civil Service Commission. This gives them a measure of independence, which they prize highly. The Inspectorate is nowadays recruited, by public advertisement, almost exclusively from the teaching profession. It is headed by a Senior Chief Inspector (SCI), who is responsible to the Permanent Secretary. Directly under the SCI are six Chief Inspectors, who deal jointly with national matters, and have individual responsibility for one or more of the following:

Primary and Secondary Education.
Special Education, Community Homes, Independent Schools,
    External Relations.
Vocational Further Education.
Non-vocational Further Education.
Training of Teachers.
Educational Research and Development.

For purposes of inspection England is divided into nine geographical divisions; for each of these a Divisional Inspector is responsible. Each division is divided into districts, to each of which an Inspector is allotted. All HMI in the field work both as individuals and, when called upon, as members of divisional or national teams. These HMI are moved every few years from one district to another, so that they may gain wide experience. Divisional Inspectors are similarly moved. At the DES there is a corps of about fifty Staff Inspectors, each specializing in some particular field of educational work: for example, the teaching of chemistry, rural education, buildings and equipment, or liaison with other countries.

There is a separate Inspectorate for Wales, with a structure similar to the English one but simpler, as the country is a single unit, with no divisions. At its head is a Chief Inspector. On primary and secondary education it reports to the Secretary of State for Wales.

On paper the functions of HMI do not appear to be greatly different from those of school inspectors in many other countries.

"The function of Her Majesty's Inspectors," says the Department's pamphlet on *How DES is organised*,[11] "is to maintain a comprehensive knowledge of the educational system, to assess the efficiency of it and to offer advice on all aspects of education to the officers of the Department, to local education authorities and to the staff and heads of educational establishments."

There is, however, a fundamental difference between the way in which these functions are interpreted in this country from that in which similar functions are interpreted in many others. In brief, HMI may not give orders, either to LEAs or to teachers; they may only criticize, commend, and advise. They carry out their inspectorial functions rigorously and efficiently. They may be highly critical. But there the Inspectors' duty ends; it is the duty of those in charge of the school to decide whether the criticisms made are justified, and if so what must be done to put matters right. Any teacher who is adversely criticized in an HMI report must be shown the criticism and given an opportunity to answer it. On the other hand, an Inspector's report may not be altered by anyone other than the writer – not even by the Secretary of State.

Another point to be noted is that HMI have creative as well as inspectorial functions. They do much in-service training, especially in the DES programme of short courses for teachers, for which they are responsible. The leaders of these courses are usually Staff Inspectors, but any HMI with relevant knowledge or skill may be called upon to act as a lecturer or tutor. The Inspectorate is also largely responsible for compiling the admirable series of booklets on educational matters which the DES publishes for the help and guidance of teachers, pupils, students, parents, and the general public. Finally, the importance of their function as liaison officers between the DES and the other parts of the educational system can hardly be exaggerated. They sit as 'observers' or 'assessors' (members without voting powers) on immumerable councils, boards, and committees, and on these, and in less formal discussions, do invaluable service as go-betweens.

Local Education Authorities

By Section 7 of the Education Act 1944 it is the statutory duty of the LEA:

> . . .so far as their powers extend, to contribute towards the spiritual, moral, mental, and physical development of the community by securing that

efficient education . . . shall be available to meet the needs of the population of their area.

That duty remains unaltered under the Local Government Act 1972.

From 1944 to 1964 there were 146 LEAs in England and Wales: 129 in England and 17 in Wales. They were the councils of the 62 administrative counties, the councils of the 83 county boroughs, and one Joint Board representative of a county council and a county borough council. Various reorganizations of local government areas, especially in and around London, had by 1970 raised the number to 164.

The Local Government Act 1972 reduced the number of LEAs to 104: ninety-six in England and eight in Wales. It ended the statutory right of county borough councils to be LEAs, and abolished the divisional executives that had functioned in many county areas. It replaced the structure of counties and county boroughs by one of Metropolitan and Non-Metropolitan Counties, both divided into Districts. There are six Metropolitan Counties, all in England: Greater Manchester, Merseyside, West Midlands, South Yorkshire, West Yorkshire, Tyne and Wear. In these there are 36 Districts, whose councils are the LEAs for their areas. There are 47 Non-Metropolitan counties: 39 in England and eight in Wales. In these the county council is the LEA.

The Greater London area, which had been reorganized in 1963, and the Isles of Scilly were excluded from the 1972 reorganization. So from 1 April 1974, when the Local Government Act 1972 came into operation, the LEAs in England and Wales have been the councils of:

39 Non-Metropolitan counties in England
 8 Non-Metropolitan counties in Wales
36 Metropolitan Districts, all in England
20 Outer London Boroughs
 1 Inner London Education Authority (ILEA)[12]

As previously, the Councils of the Counties (and of the new Districts) are representative bodies elected by the ratepayers of their areas to handle all matters of local government. Their members are not necessarily all of them well acquainted with educational affairs. So Parliament decided in 1972 (though not without much argument) to keep the Education Committee a statutory committee, with the powers accorded to it by Part II of the First Schedule to the Education Act 1944. This lays down that every LEA must "establish such education committees as they think it expedient to establish for the efficient discharge of their functions with respect to education". In practice – again, as previously – the LEA appoints one Education Committee, which appoints sub-committees to consider specified areas, e.g. schools, FE, and report to it. The conditions governing the membership and functions of Education Committees laid down in the 1944 Act have also been retained: (1) "At least a majority of every education committee of a local education authority shall be members of the authority", (2) "Every education committee of a local education authority shall include persons of experience in education and persons acquainted with the educational conditions prevailing in the area for which the committee acts", and (3) "A local education authority may authorise an education committee of the authority to exercise on their behalf any of their functions with respect to education, except the power to borrow money or to raise a rate."[13] Councils differ in the degree of delegation which they confer upon their education committees; some leave almost all decisions to their committees, being content with formally approving their actions, while others allow their committees to make recommendations only, which have to be approved by the council before they can be acted upon. A practice being increasingly adopted is that of 'corporate management', whereby the policy and proposed decisions of a committee are subject to scrutiny, and co-ordination, by a body representative of all the committees.

Most county and district councils are elected on party political grounds. This naturally has its effect upon local, and indirectly upon national, educational policy, though it must be remembered that while decisions on policy within their area are the concern of the LEA, all local authorities have to work within the framework of national policy. Moreover, any projects involving large expenditure must be approved by the Secretary of State if they are to qualify for grant.

Every LEA maintains an education office staffed by salaried employees who are local government servants. This is organized on somewhat similar lines to the DES, with a Chief Education Officer (often called the Director of Education) in charge, and a hierarchy of administrative, executive, and clerical staff. It is arranged in sections, for Primary, Secondary, and Further education, and so on. Each LEA must by law appoint a Chief Education Officer (CEO). Between 1944 and 1974 LEAs had to submit their short list of candidates for the post of CEO to the Secretary of State, who had the power to veto any name; but this power was removed by the Local Government Act 1972. The CEO is assisted by Deputy and Assistant Education Officers, and by advisers or 'Organizers' whose job it is to assist teachers by advice on their class duties, particularly in such highly specialized subjects as art, drama, music, and physical education. Some LEAs employ inspectors; these, it must be noted, are not members of Her Majesty's Inspectorate. Under the Local Government Act 1972 LEAs may appoint Area Education Officers to be responsible for the administration of specified areas in Non-Metropolitan counties. Under the Employment and Training Act 1973 they must appoint a Careers Officer, to be responsible for their Careers Service.

An LEA functions in all material respects like any other body for local government. Matters for decision are brought before the education committee, referred to the appropriate sub-committee (or they may originate there), which discusses them and makes recommendations to the main committee, which approves, rejects, or modifies them. If the main committee's decision is about matters delegated to the education committee, it is reported to the council; if not, it has to be considered by the council as the authority. Matters involving expenditure of money necessitate the concurrence of the council's finance committee – which can often be a thorn in the flesh of the education committee, as the latter's expenditure is today by far the largest item in the council's budget, and therefore especially vulnerable when economies are being made.

Throughout all the education committee's deliberations technical information and professional advice are supplied by its salaried officers, who can exercise a profound influence on an LEA's policy. It is no exaggeration to say that this has often been largely created and carried through by the CEO, though ultimately he has no power in his own right. That lies with the authority, the elected council, and, as more than one forceful CEO discovered to his dismay in recent years, even the most apparently docile education committee or council may on occasion take the bit between its teeth and go its own way regardless of his advice. Where corporate management obtains, a CEO's influence can be severely restricted.

DES and LEA

It is impossible in a few paragraphs to describe comprehensively the numerous ways in which contact is maintained between the DES and the LEA. It is close, continuous, and as a rule cordial; and it is maintained by both formal and informal means. A great deal of local authority business is handled in the DES by Territorial teams, which keep in day-to-day touch with the LEAs in a given region. An important part of their task is to ensure that statutory requirements are met when, for example, schools are opened, closed, enlarged, or changed in character. There are also what are called 'Functional' teams; these deal with a wide variety of specialized matters, ranging from nursery education and school transport to new legislation.

There are many other means of contact. Discussions and consultations, both formal and informal, take place between representatives of the LEA and of particular branches in the DES, and in these the district or divisional HMI will frequently act as intermediary. When a dispute arises between an LEA and the DES which cannot be resolved in informal discussions there are various recognized forms of action which can be taken. If, for example, an LEA is unwilling to accept a Ministerial decision – say, about a project in its building programme – the education committee (or the council) may pass a resolution expressing dissent or disappointment. With or without this action, the committee (or council) may instruct the CEO to write to the DES putting the LEA's case, or to seek an opportunity to put it verbally, or, if the matter seems serious enough, to ask the Secretary of State to receive a deputation from the authority. If an LEA feels the matter to be one of general, or national, concern it may ask one, or more, of the professional associations of local government administrators to take the matter up. There is a constant flow of correspondence about such matters between these bodies and the DES. From the other side, the Secretary of State may send to an LEA a formal letter deprecating some action, or proposed action, on its part, or one advising against such action, or he may send an official down to discuss the matter with the authority.

Whenever possible the use of such formal methods of communication is preceded by informal discussions. What happens frequently is that the local authority's CEO gets on to the telephone to the appropriate officer at the DES and says "Look here, we are proposing to do so-and-so; what do you feel about it?" Or from the other end a DES officer rings up to say "I understand your Authority is proposing to do so-and-so; well, our opinion is . . ." Such informal interchange often takes place also in between the exchange of formal correspondence; the DES officer will ring through to say "I shall be sending you shortly a letter about so-and-so, and this is what I am going to say, and this is what it really means". Or the CEO will telephone "We are sending you such and such a proposal; I thought you'd like to know in advance about it, so that you can be thinking it over".

The frequency, and success, of such informal relationships depend very largely upon the personality of the local authority's CEO. When, as is often the case, he is working hand-in-glove with an experienced and knowledgeable chairman of the education committee of equal force of personality, the two together can work wonders.

Similar methods of consultation are employed in dealings between the LEA and minor authorities or voluntary organizations.

Managers and Governors

Between 1944 and 1974 it was possible for county councils to divide the whole or part of their area into 'divisions', and to delegate the administration of Primary and Secondary education in these to 'divisional executives'. There were two kinds of divisions, because the Education Act 1944 gave municipal boroughs and urban district councils with populations of 60,000 upwards, or at least 7,000 pupils on the rolls of their maintained schools, the right to claim 'excepted district' status. Divisional executives of excepted districts could draft their own scheme of administration, instead of having it made for them by the LEA, and they might be conceded some share of the administration of FE within their division. No divisional executive, however, had the power to borrow money or raise a rate. The number of divisional executives varied over the years between about 200 and 160; in 1974 there were 30 excepted districts and 142 other divisional executives.

The Local Government Act 1972 abolished divisional executives. Although under that Act LEAs may appoint officers to carry out various tasks in specified districts, and committees to advise them, there is currently no intermediate administrative body between the education committee of the LEA and the managers and governors of schools.

Section 17 of the Education Act 1944 requires that every maintained Primary school shall have a properly constituted board of managers, working in accordance with rules of management, and every maintained Secondary school a properly constituted board of governors, working according to articles of government. A board of management may not consist of fewer than six persons; no minimum figure is specified for a board of governors, and these boards are normally larger than boards of managers. For a County Primary school the entire board is appointed by the LEA. For a Voluntary Controlled school two-thirds of the managers or governors are appointed by the LEA, and one-third by the body owning the school premises; for a Voluntary Aided or Special Agreement school the proportions are reversed. By Section 20 of the Education Act 1944 several schools may be grouped together under a single board of managers or governors; this is frequently done.

The statutory powers granted to boards of governors and managers of County schools are extremely limited. Unless invited by the authority to take part, these boards have no control over the appointment of teachers to their schools. Boards of Voluntary Controlled and Special Agreement schools have a voice in the appointment of 'reserved' teachers, that is, teachers appointed specifically to give religious instruction; but none (at least officially) in the dismissal of any teacher. For Aided schools the rules of management or articles of government must specify the respective powers of appointment of the LEA and the managers or governors, which are in brief that the latter appoint and the former decide how many shall be employed. The right of dismissal rests with the LEA, except in the case of teachers appointed to give denominational religious instruction, who may be dismissed by the managers or governors for failing to give this instruction 'efficiently and suitably'.

Beyond this point it is impossible to generalize, because both LEAs and voluntary bodies vary widely in the amount of actual power they accord to boards of managers or governors. Usually, managers get less than governors. In January 1975 *Education*, in one of its 'Digests', said that "governors normally have several specific functions":

> They are usually expected to make or contribute to the appointment of head, teachers, ancillaries and other non-teaching staff, to consider questions of staff and pupil discipline, particularly cases where dismissal of staff or suspension of pupils is a possibility, and to submit estimates or recommendations for expenditure.

However limited its official power, an interested and active board of managers or governors can in other ways be very helpful to a school: by supporting and encouraging the Head Teacher and the staff, by appearing at school open days, concerts, and suchlike 'occasions', and by acting as advocate for the school with the LEA.

In 1975 the Secretary of State appointed a committee of enquiry, under the chairmanship of Mr Tom Taylor, leader of the Blackburn Council:

> To review the arrangements for the management and government of maintained primary and secondary schools in England and Wales, including the composition and functions of bodies of managers and governors, and their

relationships with local education authorities, with head teachers and staffs of schools, with parents of pupils and with the local community at large; and to make recommendations.

This enquiry was still in progress at the end of 1976.

The Head Teacher

Like all other bodies exercising administrative control in English education, boards of managers and governors do not interfere with the day–to–day organization of the school life or with the curriculum and teaching methods. These are held to be the responsibility of the Head Teacher, who is accorded more power and more freedom in the use of it than the heads of schools in any other country known to the writer. This is primarily due to the conviction with which two beliefs are still very generally held in this country: first, that the best way in which to ensure good results is to vest responsibility for a job in a person and then to allow him to go about it in his own way, intervening only if he is manifestly not doing it properly; and secondly, that a school is not only a place for learning but also a society, free to plan and conduct its corporate life as seems best to it, provided that it keeps this life within the accepted framework laid down by social convention and the national policy for education. The Head Teacher's task is, in partnership with his staff and his pupils, to create such an autonomous society, and to maintain it in a state of good health.

Further Education

The law relating to the government of FE colleges maintained by LEAs is laid down in the Education (No. 2) Act 1968. As in the case of schools, there must be an instrument of government for each college, and every college must be conducted in accordance with articles of government. There is also the same provision that, provided the Secretary of State agrees, two or more colleges may be looked after by a single governing body. The Act implies staff participation in government; the articles of government are to "determine the functions to be exercised respectively, in relation to the institution, by the local education authority, the body of governors, the principal, and the academic board, if any".

The Act does not apply to voluntary colleges. It does, however, specify the mode of government for Special schools maintained by LEAs. In general, the terms resemble those for county schools.

References

1 On 1 April the Minister of Education became the Secretary of State for Education and Science.

2 Education Act 1944, Section 5.
3 ibid, Section 112.
4 Ordinarily, questions in a particular field (e.g. education) are all taken together on one day each week.
5 Education Act 1944, Section 25.
6 ibid, Section 1 (2).
7 ibid, Section 1 (1). (Author's italics.)
8 Local Government Manpower Committee, Second Report, 1951. HMSO.
9 The required Regulations were about Standards for School Premises, Primary and Secondary schools, Further Education, Local Education Authorities, Provision of Milk and Meals, School Health Service, Handicapped Pupils, Scholarships and Other Benefits, Training of Teachers.
10 By HM Stationery Office, 49 High Holborn, London WCIV 6HB.
11 1974 edition, p. 10. The booklet is available from the DES, Elizabeth House, York Road, London SEI 7PH.
12 The Inner London Education Authority (ILEA) is unique, being neither a County nor a District Council. It consists of 48 members: the 35 Greater London Council (GLC) members elected for inner London, plus one representative of each of the 12 inner London Borough Councils and of the Common Council of the City of London. It works through an Education Committee consisting of the 48 members of the Authority, plus 16 members chosen for their experience in education.
13 Education Act 1944, First Schedule, Part II.
14 Education Act 1944, First Schedule, Part III, as amended by the Education Act 1946, Second Schedule.

Further reading

ALEXANDER, SIR WILLIAM, *Education in England*. Newnes Educational, 2nd edition, 1964.
ALEXANDER, LORD, and TAYLOR, GEORGE, *County and Voluntary Schools*. Councils and Education Press, 5th edition, 1977.
BARON, GEORGE, and HOWELL, D. A., *Government and Management of Schools*. Athlone Press, 1974.
BARRELL, G. R., *Teachers and the Law*. Methuen, 4th edition, 1975. *Legal Cases for Teachers*. Methuen, 1970.
BLACKIE, JOHN, *Inspecting and the Inspectorate*. Routledge & Kegan Paul, 1970.
BOYLE, EDWARD, and CROSLAND, ANTHONY, in conversation with KOGAN, MAURICE, *The Politics of Education*. Penguin, 1971.
DENT, H. C., *The Education Act 1944*. University of London Press, 12th edition, 1968.
GOSDEN, P. H. J. H., *The Development of Educational Administration in England and Wales*. Blackwell, 1966.
LAWRENCE, BERNARD, *The Administration of Education in Britain*. Batsford, 1972.
REGAN, D. E., *Local Government and Education*. Allen & Unwin, 1977.
SMITH, W. O. LESTER, *Government of Education*. Penguin, Revised edition, 1968.
TAYLOR, G., and SAUNDERS, J. B., *The New Law of Education*. Butterworth, 8th edition, 1977.
VAIZEY, JOHN, *The Control of Education*. Faber, 1963.

Official

DES *Reports on Education* (gratis). They include reports on DES, LEAs, and HMI. *Schools Council. The First Three Years 1964–7.* HMSO, 1968.

Education, when the journal of the AEC, published the Minutes of the executive committee of this association, which gave a useful insight into some of the modes of consultation and negotiation between the DES and the LEAs.

| Primary Education

Section 8(1) of the Education Act 1944 defines primary education baldly as "education suitable to the requirements of junior pupils", and Section 114 explains that a 'junior pupil' is "a child who has not attained the age of twelve years". Not long after the Act came into operation, however, the Grammar schools pointed out that because of the latter definition some intellectually able children were being kept in the Primary school beyond an age at which they were ready to undertake secondary studies. The definition of primary education was consequently amended by Section 3 of the Education (Miscellaneous Provisions) Act 1948 to read:

> . . .full-time education suitable to the requirements of junior pupils who have not attained the age of ten years six months, and full-time education suitable to the requirements of junior pupils who have attained that age and whom it is expedient to educate together with junior pupils who have not attained that age.

This, together with the definition of 'junior pupil' given above, meant in plain English that primary education might be concluded as early as the age of ten years six months and must be concluded before the twelfth birthday.

The Education Act 1964 however, empowered LEAs, and non-statutory bodies, to establish schools with different age-limits from the above. Section 1 states that proposals may:

> specify an age which is below the age of ten years and six months and an age which is above the age of twelve years.

The 1964 Act is permissive only; there is no statutory obligation to establish schools along the lines it suggests. It has given birth to the 'Middle' school, which, with an age range of eight to twelve, nine to thirteen, or, occasionally, ten to fourteen, may be designated either Primary or Secondary. Of about 1,150 Middle schools in 1976 about four out of ten were Primary.

Section 35 of the 1944 Act defines 'compulsory school age' as "any age between five and fifteen years". This is interpreted to mean that primary education is compulsory from the beginning of the school term next after the child's fifth birthday. But Section 8 of the Act requires the LEAs to "have regard":

to the need for securing that provision is made for pupils who have not attained the age of five years by the provision of Nursery schools or, where the authority consider the provision of such schools to be inexpedient, by the provision of nursery classes in other schools.

Nursery Schools and Classes

A child may enter a Nursery school at the age of two, a nursery class at three. In 1976 there were about 45,000 children attending Nursery schools or classes for the whole day, and 113,000 for part of the day. (Nursery classes are classes in Primary schools equipped for nursery education.) These figures represent only about ten per cent of children between two and five. That the numbers were so small was partly due to the continuous pressure imposed upon the LEAs for many years after 1944 by the necessity to provide sufficient accommodation for the increasing number of children of 'compulsory school age'. In 1960 the Minister of Education advised against any further expansion of Nursery education.[1] In October 1968, however, the Secretary of State announced an 'Urban Programme' of development in which, during the first four years from his announcement, £20 million to £25 million would be spent on providing Nursery schools and classes, day nurseries and children's homes in areas with:

(i) more than two per cent of households with more than $1\frac{1}{2}$ persons per room (on the 1966 census); and/or

(ii) more than six per cent of immigrants.

By 1975 this had resulted in the provision of about 24,000 additional places.

Nursery education is one of the happiest and most enlightened features of English education. There are no formal lessons; in a specially designed environment the children occupy themselves with indoor and outdoor play, choosing freely from the wide variety of toys and other material provided; with drawing, painting, and modelling; with listening to stories told by the teacher; with singing nursery rhymes and simple songs, and dancing with gay abandon and pleasing rhythm to music; with learning to realize the values of money, weights and measures through playing at shops and practising domestic chores. It is a period of attitude and habit formation, with as much attention paid to social behaviour and physical health as to preparation for more academic learning.

A Nursery school must be in the charge of a qualified superintendent teacher. The permitted maximum number of children in a Nursery school class, or in a nursery class, is thirty – ten fewer than in Infant and Junior schools. Because of the demand for places, many children attend for one session a day only. All Nursery schools provide milk and meals.

Infants and Juniors

Except where there are Middle schools, the period between five and twelve is ordinarily divided into two stages, of infant and junior education. The infant stage ends between the ages of seven and eight. The junior stage is rather longer; for some children it may extend over a full four years. Sometimes these two stages are conducted in separate buildings, but more often in separate departments in the same building. Except in the smallest schools, where it is impossible, the infants are put in a different room (or rooms) from the juniors. Where infant and junior departments are in the same building there may or may not be an independent Head Teacher for the infants' department; generally speaking, where the departments are large there is, where they are small there is one Head Teacher for the whole Primary school, and he or she will normally teach in the Junior department. In 1976 all the Infant and First schools were co-educational, and were staffed almost entirely by women. A few Junior schools were single-sex, but the overwhelming majority were co-educational. In co-educational Junior schools the Head Teacher may be a man or a woman, and the staff invariably includes both men and women. In boys' Junior schools there are not infrequently some women teachers, usually taking the younger children, or such specialist subjects as music and art. Men teachers are rarely found in girls' Junior schools. The numbers of pupils in Primary schools vary enormously; from fewer than twenty children in a single teacher school to occasional huge schools of over 800 pupils. But for many years about half the schools have had between 100 and 300 pupils.

The Infant School

Life in the first year of the Infant school is often very similar to that in a Nursery school; but the range of material is somewhat more pedagogical, and the children's occupations – other than spontaneous play, which is continued – tend to be slightly more organized and systematized.

> For the five-year-olds the emphasis is upon a widening experience of the world in which they live. There are opportunities for experimenting with materials like sand, water, clay, paint and wood; for building with bricks and boxes; for imaginative play, for first-hand experience of living things; for enjoying stories and music; and, since children are encouraged to talk about what they see and do, there is a growing use of words.
>
> Occasions for reading, writing, and number often arise from these activities . . .[2]

In a 'Reception' class for newly-entered five-year olds, and often in other Infant school classes, there is no formal syllabus. The teacher supervises an 'Integrated Day', in which the children work individually or in small groups on various activities: drawing, painting, modelling, cutting and pasting, reading, writing, figuring, and so on. From time to time they change from one activity to another, as interest ebbs, or the teacher judges it wise. She will every now and then gather the class together for collective activities: singing or dancing,

Infants having a mid-day meal at school

for example, and for the story she will tell them at the end of the school day.

When working on these lines the Infant teacher has no more difficult educational task than that of maintaining a just balance between free activity and systematic learning, especially of the '3 Rs'. To aid the latter, many teachers fill their classrooms with a wealth of illustrative materials – much of it made by themselves and/or the children – designed to persuade children to want to read, to write, and to calculate: pictures of familiar objects with their names printed alongside them, clock faces, calendars, daily 'news' sheets compiled from information offered by the children. As in the Nursery school, the formation of good habits of health, personal hygiene, and social relations, is given much attention.

To facilitate informal methods of teaching and learning, in recent years many Primary schools have been built on the 'Open Plan' system, that is, without enclosed classrooms, the interior area of the building being divided into spaces, of various sizes and shapes, and equipped for different kinds of activities. Not all teachers are convinced of the superiority of the Open Plan building, and many would perhaps prefer a compromise incorporating some classrooms and some Open Plan spaces.

The Junior School

In a memorable passage in their report on the *Primary School*, published in 1931, the Consultative Committee of the Board of Education wrote:

> . . . At the age when they attend the Primary schools, children are active and inquisitive, delighting in movement, in small tasks that they can perform with deftness and skill, and in the sense of visible and tangible accomplishment which such tasks offer; intensely interested in the character and purpose – the shape, form, colour and use – of the material objects around them; at once absorbed in creating their own miniature world of imagination and emotion, and keen observers who take pleasure in reproducing their observations by speech and dramatic action; and still engaged in mastering a difficult and unfamiliar language . . . These activities are not aimless, but form the process by which children grow.[3]

Because of these characteristics of pre-adolescent children the Committee concluded that the curriculum offered them in school should be "thought of in terms of activity and experience rather than of knowledge to be acquired and facts to be stored". Its aim, they said, should be:

> to develop in a child the fundamental human powers and to awaken him to the fundamental interests of civilized life so far as these powers and interests lie within the compass of childhood, to encourage him to attain gradually to that control and orderly management of his energies, impulses, and emotions, which is the essence of moral and intellectual discipline, to help him to discover the idea of duty and to ensue it, and to open out his imagination and his sympathies in such a way that he may be prepared to understand and to follow in later years the highest examples of excellence in life and conduct.[4]

The history of the Junior school since 1931 has been largely that of working out in practice the ideas set down in the Consultative Committee's report. Not always successfully; during the early years many teachers took the sentence about 'activity and experience' to mean that they need not worry whether their children acquired any knowledge, so long as they remained happily busy. This gave 'Activity' methods a bad reputation, from which they have never completely recovered. But though occasional instances still occur of uncritical reliance upon activity, most Junior school teachers now endeavour – often with great success – to maintain a just balance between knowledge, skill, activity, and experience. The following quotations from an essay written by a Sheffield teacher[5] give a very good idea of enlightened Junior school practice in the 1960s:

> The physical education . . . should provide opportunities for throwing, climbing, building, dancing, etc., so that new skills can be learnt and old ones perfected. . . .
> Primary school children are curious about the world in which they live;

how clocks work, why the sky is blue, what makes the leaves fall. . . . It is vital that this spirit of inquiry should not be thwarted but fostered, for it is a sign of the rapid mental development taking place and is an invaluable educational aid. . . .

A great deal of individual work is done. . . . situations are produced so that children can only attain their objective by being able to read, or write, or do a particular type of calculation. The work is related to the everyday life of the children, who are realists, keen to discover about the world in which they live, but have no use for learning without a purpose, no use for inert ideas.

Attention should be given to speech throughout. . . . Dramatic work is an opportunity to extend and improve speech, but the example of speech which the teacher sets is probably the greatest factor in producing clarity, correct pronunciation, and pleasant intonation in the speech of the children . . . every lesson is a speech-training lesson. . . .

Practically all children except those who are backward or retarded should be able to read for information and pleasure, and have 'developed the habit of reading' before they leave the Primary school. The backward readers will need special teaching of a remedial nature . . . because the difficulties of learning to read increase greatly as the child gets older.

All children should be able to write simple letters, accounts of school journeys, or diaries, and attempt creative writing, such as adventure stories, plays, or poems. The writing should not necessarily be an end in itself but be correlated with other subjects. The methods of teaching spelling, grammar, and punctuation will depend upon the class, but their purpose should be that the written work shall be intelligible and interesting.

The rate of progress at mathematics will depend on the ability of the children, but by the time they reach the end of the Junior school they should know the fundamental rules and have a knowledge of geometrical forms. It is most important that the mathematics should be based on the everyday life of the children, and the mathematical concepts arrived at by counting, handling money, and measuring with scales, clocks, rulers, etc.

Children of this age are sensitive to beauty, and the aesthetic experiences of music, poetry, art, and drama are of great value, not only from the pleasure they give but by enriching the child's personality. Often an aesthetic experience in childhood is responsible for the awakening of latent talent.

Art and craft work, though often carried out as ends in themselves, are more usually an extension of work done in another subject.

This teacher pointed out, quite rightly, that the handling of these subjects becomes more difficult towards the end of the primary stage, because children then "tend to become critical of their own efforts". So it is the task of the teacher:

by the use of new media and by a careful but stimulating approach, to help them to use their more mature judgement and skill without losing all spontaneity and creativeness. . . .

Much of the success of good Primary school teaching, said the writer, has been due to recognition of the principle that:

> Good emotional development is essential during the period of childhood. . . . The most important way of ensuring the good emotional development of the children is to have a class teacher who is stable and mature in character, capable of sympathy and understanding without becoming involved in emotional conflicts.

Since that essay was written Primary school practice has developed considerably, thanks to the skill and devotion of many teachers, to large-scale experiments and research projects mounted by the Nuffield Foundation, the NFER, the Schools Council, and Institutes of Education, and to the spread of new techniques such as team teaching and the use of media resource centres.

It should be remembered that Primary education (as the term is understood today; in the 19th century it was merely a synonym for Elementary education) is entirely a 20th century concept. It began to emerge in the early 1920s, and was first given official recognition in the 1926 Report of the Consultative Committee of the Board of Education on *The Education of the Adolescent*, which proposed that all schooling up to the age of eleven should be considered Primary education, and all schooling thereafter Secondary education. What should be done in the Primary stage was set out in detail in two subsequent Reports by the Committee: *The Primary School* (1931), and *Infant and Nursery Schools* (1933).

Most of the advice offered in the 1931 Report was for the good of the Junior school; but one proposal – though made with the best of intentions – was not.

> In view of the varying attainments of children it is specially important that there should be small classes or groups. Where classes are rather large, the task of the teacher will be lightened if the pupils are carefully classified according to their capacity . . . in very large primary schools there might, wherever possible, be a triple track system of organization: a series of "A" classes or groups for the bright children, and a series of smaller "C" classes or groups to include retarded children, both series being parallel to the ordinary series of "B" classes or groups for the average children.[6]

Such 'streaming' quickly became widespread, and, despite the Consultative Committee's warning, not infrequently extended down into the Infant school. The reason was only too sadly clear. Once the principle of Primary and Secondary stages of education was accepted, it became an important function of the Primary school to prepare children for entry into the Secondary stage. But there were not enough places in the recognized Secondary (i.e. Grammar) schools for all the children thought capable of academic work; so competition for the available places became severe. Junior school teachers found themselves increasingly under pressure from ambitious parents, and in all too many cases succumbed to it, and gave more and more attention to the "A" stream, the potential winners of 'the scholarship', as it was called, to the detriment of the "B" and

Juniors weaving as part of a history project

"C" streams. And so, as the Government's White Paper, *Educational Reconstruction*, which preceded the Education Act 1944, had to admit:

> Instead of the Junior schools performing their proper and highly important function of fostering the potentialities of children at an age when their minds are nimble and receptive, their curiosity strong, their imagination fertile and their spirits high, the curriculum is too often cramped and distorted by over-emphasis on examination subjects and on ways and means of defeating the examiners. The blame for this rests not with the teachers but with the system. [7]

Though the 'system' was radically altered by the Education Act 1944 which abolished 'Elementary' education and introduced Secondary education for all children, parental pressure persisted and indeed intensified, because it was no longer possible to get into the Grammar school by paying tuition fees. And so, alas! some Primary schools continued to allow their curriculum to be 'cramped and distorted by over-emphasis on examination subjects'. As Secondary Modern schools began during the 1950s to offer increasingly attractive courses, and in particular courses leading to the General Certificate of Education (GCE), this pressure from parents tended to diminish somewhat, but remained strong enough in many places to prevent full realization of the ideal aimed at by the Consultative Committee in its 1931 Report, that the Primary school curriculum should be regarded as "not only consisting of lessons to be mastered but as providing fields of new and interesting experience to be explored"[8]

Despite the 'Eleven-plus' examination (described in the next chapter) a growing number of Junior schools were during the 1950s and 1960s providing increasingly wide and liberal curricula, making extensive use of individual and group methods of learning, encouraging initiative, activity, and enterprise in their pupils, giving them a great deal of freedom to determine the jobs they would do, the ways in which they would carry them out, and the speed at which they would work. This approach, which in the 1970s came in for some harsh criticism, is based on the belief that the development of children's potential ability through 'activity and experience' – skilfully supervised and guided – is more important than the accumulation of knowledge: though good teachers are always keenly aware that it is essential for their pupils to acquire a mastery of basic knowledge and learning skills while still in Primary school.

The Middle School

The first Middle schools were opened in the West Riding of Yorkshire in September 1968. Thereafter their number grew, at first slowly but later more quickly. By 1976 there were about 1,150, containing over 350,000 pupils. Most of these covered the age range 9–13, and nearly six out of ten had been officially designated Secondary schools. Nine out of ten of these, and all the schools designated Primary, were co-educational.

Curricula varied according to the age of entry and the school's designation. But the following principles seemed to be observed by practically all Middle schools:

(1) A foreign language must be taught;
(2) There must be elementary laboratory facilities for science;
(3) There must be specialist areas for the teaching of craft subjects;
(4) Because of the foregoing requirements, a proportion of the teaching staff must be specialists.

References

1 Circular 8/60, dated 31 May 1960.

2 Reports on Education. No. 1, *The Primary School*. Issued by the Ministry of Education, July 1963.
3 Page xvii. Despite its name, this Report dealt almost entirely with what is now called the Junior school. The Consultative Committee published a separate Report two years later on *Infant and Nursery Schools*.
4 Ibid., p. 93.
5 Mr R. T. Smith, then at Carterknowle Primary School, Sheffield.
6 *The Primary School* (Report of the Consultative Committee), pp. 77–78.
7 *Educational Reconstruction*, p. 6.
8 *The Primary School*, p. xviii.

Further reading

ATKINSON, MARY, *Junior School Community*. Longmans, 2nd edition, 1962.
BLACKIE, JOHN, *Inside the Primary School*. By a former Chief Inspector (Primary). H.M. Stationery Office, 1967.
BURSTALL, CLARE, with JAMIESON, MONICA, COHEN, SUSAN, and HARGREAVES, MARGARET, *Primary French in the Balance*. NFER, 1974.
DANIEL, M. V., *Activity in the Primary School*. Blackwell, 1949.
DEARDEN, R. F., *The Philosophy of Primary Education*. Routledge & Kegan Paul, 1968.
GOLDMAN, J. M., *The School in our Village*. Batsford, 1957.
MARSH, LEONARD, *Alongside the Child in the Primary School*. A. & C. Black, 1970.
ROSS, ALEXANDER M., *The Education of Childhood*. Harrap, 1960.
WHITBREAD, NANETTE, *The Evolution of the Nursery-Infant School*. Routledge & Kegan Paul, 1972.
YARDLEY, ALICE, *Reaching Out; Exploration and Language; Discovering the Physical World; Senses and Sensitivity. Young Children Thinking*. (Young Children Learning Series), Evans Bros., 1970–73.

Official

Consultative Committee of the Board of Education. *The Primary School*, 1931. *Infant and Nursery Schools*, 1933.
Ministry of Education. Seven to Eleven (Pamphlet 15). *Story of a School* (Pamphlet 14).
Primary Education. Suggestions for the consideration of teachers and others concerned with the work of Primary Schools, 1959.
Children and their Primary Schools ('Plowden' Report). Report of the Central Advisory Council for Education (England). Vol. 1, Report; Vol. 2, Research and Surveys, 1967.
Primary Education in Wales ('Gittins' Report). Report of the Central Advisory Council for Education (Wales), 1968.
Circular 2/73, *Nursery Education*, 2 February 1973. *Nursery Education*, DES 'Report on Education' No. 81, January 1975.
Towards the Middle School. Education Pamphlet 57, 1970.
Launching Middle Schools. Education Survey 8, 1970.
All from H.M. Stationery Office.

| # Secondary Education

By its organization of the statutory system of public education in three progressive stages, and by requiring that the first, the Primary stage, be concluded not later than the twelfth birthday, the Education Act 1944 made a period of full-time Secondary education compulsory for all children attending maintained and grant-aided schools. By raising the upper age-limit for compulsory full-time education from fourteen to fifteen (with provision for a later raising to sixteen) it ensured that the period of Secondary education should not be less than three years, and by permitting the education of 'senior pupils' to continue until the nineteenth birthday made it possible for any child to stay in a Secondary school for seven years, or even rather more.

Section 3 of the Education (Miscellaneous Provisions) Act 1948, by reducing the minimum age at which a child could be transferred from Primary to Secondary education to ten and a half, made possible a stay of eight and a half years in a Secondary school. Section 8 of the Education Act 1946 had made clear that a child could leave school only at the end of the term in which he attained the 'leaving age', and Section 9 of the Education Act 1962 forbade after September 1963 leaving at Christmas. The 'Middle' schools sanctioned by Section 1 of the Education Act 1964 can either shorten or lengthen the period of Secondary education, since they can be officially designated either Primary or Secondary. The raising of the school leaving age to sixteen in 1972 ensured a minimum of four years' secondary education for all.

The 1944 Act did much more than make secondary education compulsory for all children. In Section 8, after laying upon the LEAs the duty to see that in their areas there were 'sufficient' schools providing primary education and secondary education, it went on to instruct them that:

> the schools available for an area shall not be deemed to be sufficient unless they are sufficient in number, character, and equipment to afford for all pupils opportunities for education offering such variety of instruction and training as may be desirable in view of their different ages, abilities and aptitudes, and of the different periods for which they may be expected to remain at school, including practical instruction appropriate to their respective needs.

This definition imposes upon the LEAs a statutory obligation to secure the provision of different kinds of secondary education. It follows that they must devise means of discovering, so far as possible, either during the primary stage, or early in the secondary, what particular kinds of secondary education children seem most suited for. This obligation is not removed by the organization of secondary education on Comprehensive lines.

Different kinds of post-Primary schools were available in 1945. Since 1902 there had developed in England and Wales three clearly distinguishable types of post-Primary education, given in three separate groups of schools: the recognized Secondary schools (which were all 'Grammar' schools), the group of quasi-vocational schools known generically as Junior Technical schools, and the various kinds of Senior Elementary schools. In 1943 the Government, fortified by the 1938 Report of the Consultative Committee of the Board of Education (the 'Spens' Report),[1] which recommended that all three groups should be recognized as Secondary schools, and by the Report of a committee set up in 1941 by the President of the Board of Education (the 'Norwood' Report),[2] which discovered that there were three types of children ideally suited for these three kinds of education, accepted the idea of a tripartite organization of secondary education: in Grammar, Technical, and Modern schools. In doing so, however, the Government emphasized that they did not regard this arrangement as rigid and inflexible.

> "It would be wrong," they said, "to suppose that they [Grammar, Technical, and Modern schools] will necessarily remain separate and apart. Different types may be combined in one building or on one site . . . In any case the free interchange of pupils from one type of education to another must be facilitated."[3]

The Grammar schools were those which had previously been officially recognized 'Secondary' schools. The Secondary Technical schools comprised the schools previously known as Junior Technical, Junior Art, and Junior Commercial schools. The Secondary Modern schools were the promoted Elementary schools.[4]

It is difficult to see what else the Government could have done. Any large-scale reorganization of the schools would inevitably have delayed the introduction of secondary education for all, even had there been agreement about how to reorganize. But there was not; the only alternative proposal, to provide secondary education in 'Multilateral' or 'Comprehensive' schools taking all the children in a given geographical area, was distasteful to the majority of professional and public opinion, had never been tried in this country, and had been firmly rejected by the 'Spens' Committee – except on an experimental basis in favourable circumstances.[5] It would in any case have demanded a building programme quite beyond the country's capacity at the time.

But, most unhappily, for many years these three groups of schools had been accorded by the public very different degrees of esteem. The Grammar school stood easily highest, as the gateway giving access to professional and executive rank in employment. The Junior Technical school – usually entered at twelve or thirteen – was regarded as a 'second-best' for those who had failed to secure one of the coveted Grammar school places. The Senior Elementary school was the school in which remained those who were deemed not capable of, or who were uninterested in, more advanced education. The educational implications were inextricably entangled with social and economic implications; the Grammar school was regarded not only as socially superior to the Junior Technical school, but also as economically superior, because it led to better-paid and (a crucial point in the years of widespread unemployment between the two World Wars) more secure employment. The Junior Technical school, giving entry into skilled trades, had some evident (but not so highly prized) economic and social advantages. The Senior Elementary school offered none of these advantages, and consequently stood much the lowest in public esteem.

Just as there were different kinds of Secondary schools already available in 1945, so there were established means of determining the capacity of children to undertake the education given in one of them: the Grammar school. Ever since the introduction in 1907 of the 'free place' system, whereby a fixed proportion (usually 25 per cent) of the annual entry into maintained Secondary schools had to be pupils from Elementary schools whose tuition fees were paid by their LEAs, the authorities had been constantly refining and improving the techniques by which they selected children for the award of scholarships to the Grammar school. From 1945 onwards this selection machinery was adapted to serve as the means of allocating children to appropriate Secondary schools.

Again, it is difficult to see what else the LEAs could have done. Thanks principally to the introduction (as early as the 1920s), and the progressive refinement, of standardized objective tests of 'intelligence', and later of attainment in formal English and arithmetic, the selection techniques in general use in 1945 constituted the most accurate instrument known for predicting capacity to undertake Grammar school studies: and they were continually being further refined. Nevertheless, during the following years the 'Eleven-plus', as the selection process became known, was the cause of more anxiety, frustration and disappointment than any other feature in the English educational system: in fact, it would hardly be an exaggeration to say than all the other features combined.

This is not the place to examine in detail the reasons for the distress caused by the Eleven-plus to parents and their children; that was done thoroughly and objectively many years ago in a report[6] edited by Professor Philip Vernon, a leading authority on the matter. But without realizing that such distress did occur on a very large scale, it is not possible to understand fully the trend towards Comprehensive organization of Secondary education during the 1950s and early 1960s.

As secondary education became increasingly organized on Comprehensive lines the incidence of the Eleven-plus decreased. But as late as 1977 children were taking it. (Only in this year did the ILEA, an out-and-out Comprehensive authority, get completely rid of it.) A brief description of it is therefore given.

The Eleven-plus is administered by LEAs. The procedures they use vary considerably in detail but in total are broadly similar. The following are the techniques most generally employed:

(*a*) Standardized objective tests of intelligence (or 'verbal reasoning', as they are commonly called).

(*b*) Tests, usually objective and frequently standardized, of attainment in formal English and arithmetic.

These two sets of tests are usually checked by

(*c*) Reports from Primary school Head Teachers, and frequently by

(*d*) Scrutiny of records of children compiled over the period of Primary education.

A few LEAs make a regular practice of interviewing parents, but generally speaking interviews are restricted to consideration of doubtful cases.

The tests are ordinarily given (usually in February or March) to the children in their own schools, by their own teachers, who then mark the tests according to the instructions supplied to them (which allow for no personal opinions about the correctness or incorrectness of answers) and, again in accordance with instructions, convert the 'raw' scores into 'standard' scores. The scripts and the marks are then sent to the local education office, where the marks are checked, and the examinees from all the schools in the authority's area are ranged in a single order-of-merit.

An Examination Board appointed by the LEA then decides how far down this order-of-merit candidates may be allocated to Grammar schools without further consideration, and similarly, how far up from the bottom of the order the candidates may be allocated at once to Secondary Modern schools. The point at which the upper line is drawn will be largely determined by the proportionate number of Grammar school places available in the area; there is no absolute standard by which children qualify for entry into the Grammar school, and it has been a constant cause of complaint that there is great disparity between LEA areas – and districts within areas – in the provision of Grammar school places.

Ordinarily, not all the Grammar school places are allocated by this first selection; a number are reserved for 'border-zone' pupils, that is, for candidates whose names appear between the upper and the lower lines that have been drawn. A very great deal of care is given by LEAs to ensure that the most accurate allocation possible is made of the 'border-zone' candidates; specimens of their school work may be called for, additional tests given them, teachers and parents – and even occasionally the children themselves – consulted.

From the late 1950s onward growing numbers of LEAs 'abolished' the Eleven-plus: that is to say, they abandoned some of the techniques, or spread the tests over a longer period, or otherwise rendered the selection procedure more innocuous and less obvious. The rapid increase during the 1960s of Comprehensive schools expedited this process.

Types of Secondary Schools

As late as 1965 secondary education was still very largely organized on the tripartite basis of Grammar, Technical, and Modern schools. But for at least ten years previously two trends had been breaking down the original near-universality of tripartitism: the amalgamation of segregated schools into Comprehensive or Bilateral schools and the introduction into Secondary Modern schools of academic courses similar to (though less advanced than) those given in Grammar and Technical Secondary schools. In 1965 the Labour Government requested LEAs to submit plans for reorganizing their schools on Comprehensive lines.[7] In 1970 the Conservative Government rescinded the request,[8] but in 1974 the incoming Labour Government reaffirmed its policy of Comprehensive organization everywhere.[9] By 1976 there were over 3,300 Comprehensive schools, housing over 75 per cent of the pupils in maintained Secondary schools.

Bilaterals were Secondary schools "organized to provide for any two of the three main elements, i.e. Grammar, Technical, Modern, in clearly defined sides".[10] The number of 'recognized' Bilateral schools was never large, but the Bilateral schools recognized as such by the DES made up only a relatively small proportion of the schools which were in fact bilateral. The 'unrecognized' Bilaterals included the large number of Secondary Modern schools which provided a 'Grammar' course in which pupils were prepared for the examinations leading to the GCE. In the summer examination in 1965 over 1,500 Secondary Modern schools (out of 3,900) entered over 60,000 candidates for the GCE. In that year the DES ceased to include the category of Bilateral schools in its annual statistics. With it went any mention of Multilaterals, of which there had never been more than a handful.

The Comprehensive school was officially defined in 1947 (in Circular 144) as a Secondary school "intended to provide for all the secondary education of all the children in a given area without an organization in three sides". Until recently few schools were completely comprehensive in the terms of that definition. Many were single-sex schools. Many did not include all the most able children in their catchment area, because parents sent these to near-by Grammar schools, or to independent schools. Since the issue of Circular 10/65 the above definition of a Comprehensive school no longer holds good in all cases. This Circular listed "six main forms of comprehensive organization", only one of which, the 'all-through' school (age-range eleven to eighteen-plus), provides for "all the secondary education of all the children" in its area. The other forms require at least two schools to cover the period of secondary education.

This plan of breaking the secondary stage into two parts was first tried out experimentally, on a small scale, by the Leicestershire LEA in 1957. In this experiment all children went from the Primary school into a 'High School', and stayed there until the age of fourteen, or in exceptional cases thirteen. Then, the parents had to decide whether to keep their children in the High School until the end of compulsory school age (then fifteen), or have them transferred to a 'Grammar' school (with a wider curriculum than that of the traditional Grammar school), where they could stay until eighteen-plus. If the latter option was taken up, the parents had to promise to keep their children at school for at least another two years. The experiment proved successful enough to encourage the

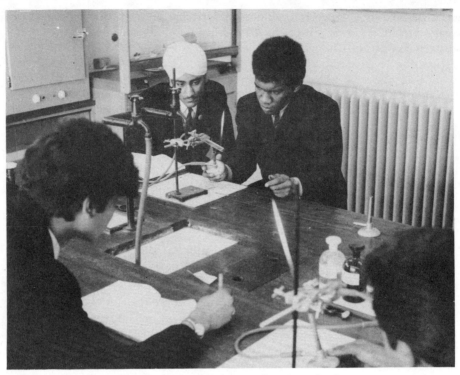

Science lesson in a comprehensive school

LEA to try it out in other districts; and within about ten years the whole of the county of Leicestershire was organized on this plan.

Circular 10/65 allowed the break to be made at thirteen, fourteen, or sixteen. The six forms of comprehensive organization which it accepted were:

(*a*) The 'all-through' Comprehensive school with an age-range of eleven to eighteen-plus.

(*b*) A two-tier system in which *all* pupils transfer at eleven to a Junior Comprehensive school, and *all* transfer at thirteen or fourteen to a Senior Comprehensive school.

(*c*) A two-tier system in which *all* pupils transfer at eleven to a Junior Comprehensive school, but only *some* transfer, at thirteen or fourteen, to a Senior school. The others remain in the Junior Comprehensive.

(*d*) A two-tier system in which *all* pupils transfer at eleven to a Junior Comprehensive school, and at thirteen or fourteen *all* can choose between two Senior schools, one terminating at or near the end of 'compulsory school age', the other going well beyond it.

(*e*) A single Comprehensive school with an age-range of eleven to sixteen, with an optional sixth form college for pupils beyond sixteen.

(*f*) A three-tier system in which *all* pupils transfer from Primary school at eight or nine to a Comprehensive Middle school, and thence at twelve or thirteen to a Comprehensive Secondary school with an age-range of twelve or thirteen to eighteen.

All these forms of organization have been tried, but up to 1976 the 'all through' Comprehensive school remained much the most numerous.

Functions of the Schools

The Grammar school is by many centuries the oldest type of secondary school in the country – it can trace its ancestry back in an unbroken line to the seventh century A.D. Its historical function has been to give an academic education which serves as a foundation for University studies. Since the establishment in 1902 of a statutory system of secondary education it has done so in maintained schools by providing:

a general course lasting for about five years in which the treatment of all subjects and groups of subjects but notably languages (classical and modern), mathematics, and science, follows a predominantly logical development; and . . . a subsequent intensive course in the 'sixth form' covering a narrower range of studies, which for many boys and girls leads naturally on to studies at the University level.[11]

"The distinguishing feature of both courses", continues the Ministry's pamphlet, "lies not so much, perhaps, in their content as in their length, in the scholarly treatment of their content, and in the stern intellectual discipline that they afford." This remains true today; consequently the Grammar school type of course is appropriate only for the intellectually able boy or girl.

The subjects normally studied in Grammar schools are English language and literature, modern foreign languages (French almost always, German frequently, Italian, Spanish, Russian, and other languages occasionally), classical languages (this usually means Latin; Greek is rare), history, geography, mathematics pure and applied (the latter not always), chemistry, physics, biology (the last more frequently in girls' schools, often to the exclusion of physics), art, music, woodwork and/or metalwork for boys, and home economics for girls. Religious education is compulsory. Physical education is given in all schools, and is supplemented by organized outdoor games, athletic sports, and as a rule swimming. In boys' schools cricket and football (usually Association) are universal, with hockey and lawn tennis as subsidiaries; in girls' schools hockey and lawn tennis are practically universal, cricket, netball and lacrosse not infrequent.

To the foregoing subjects enterprising schools will add for their older pupils one or more of engineering, technical drawing, computer education, architecture, economics, commercial subjects (usually for girls), and occasionally philosophy, psychology, and/or sociology. Some Grammar schools include gardening and a few provide an agricultural or horticultural course.

All Grammar schools prepare their pupils to take the external examinations for the GCE, and a majority of their pupils sit these examinations, ordinarily between the ages of fifteen and eighteen. The examinations are taken at two levels, Ordinary and Advanced (there are also scholarship papers, higher in standard than the Advanced). They are 'Subject' examinations, that is to say, passes are awarded on success in individual subjects, not groups of subjects, as was the case with the School Certificate which, along with the Higher School Certificate, was superseded by the GCE in 1951. A GCE can be gained by passing in one subject only at the Ordinary level; and a candidate may go on adding other subjects indefinitely, at Ordinary or Advanced level, or both. A GCE examination may not be taken by a candidate under the age of sixteen (on 1 September in that year) unless:

> the head teacher certifies that it is desirable on educational grounds to enter him earlier, and that he has pursued a course of study with such competence that it is probable he will pass the examination in the subjects for which it is proposed to enter him.[12]

Large numbers of pupils under the age of sixteen are entered, almost all of them for examinations at the Ordinary level.

A GCE carrying passes in appropriate subjects and at required levels gives exemption from University entrance examinations and from the preliminary examinations of all the main professional associations. University requirements vary with Faculties and Departments, but the absolute minimum is ordinarily a pass in four or five subjects of which two at least must be passed at the Advanced level.

The examinations for the GCE are administered by eight examining boards. Seven are University boards; the Associated Examining Board (AEB), which was established in 1953 and held its first examinations in 1955, is an independent, self-supporting company, limited by guarantee, and representative of a large number of educational, industrial, commercial, and professional institutions.

The Boards are:

Southern Universities' Joint Board for School Examinations (Universities of Bath, Bristol, Exeter, Reading, Southampton, and Surrey).

University of Cambridge Local Examinations Syndicate.

London University Entrance and School Examinations Council.

Joint Matriculation Board (Universities of Manchester, Liverpool, Leeds, Sheffield, and Birmingham).

Oxford Local Examinations.

Oxford and Cambridge Schools Examinations Board.

Welsh Joint Education Committee.

Associated Examining Board for the General Certificate in Education.

Secondary Technical Schools

The distinguishing feature of the Secondary Technical school, wrote the Ministry of Education in 1947, is:

> relationship to a particular industry or occupation or group of industries or occupations. . . . [It] caters for a minority of able children who are likely to make their best response when the curriculum is strongly coloured by [industrial or commercial] interests, both from the point of view of a career and because subject-matter of this kind appeals to them.[13]

There were always relatively few Secondary Technical schools; only 317 in 1947, as against 1,207 Grammar and 3,019 Modern schools, and the number has decreased ever since. By 1976 there were under 25. In view of the pressing national need to produce more scientists, technologists, technicians and craftsmen one might have expected new Secondary Technical schools to spring up in great numbers during the early years after the Second World War, and it is still difficult to explain confidently why this did not happen. Perhaps the fundamental reason is that a considerable body of professional opinion remained unconvinced that there was any necessity for a Secondary Technical school, as such, in the post-1944 structure of secondary education. Its critics claimed that the Grammar school could do – and did – just as well or better all the more advanced work it attempted, and that the Secondary Modern school could do – and did – just as well or better all its other work.

Secondly, the Secondary Technical school, as a selective school, had to contend with the overwhelming prestige of the Grammar school. It entered this contest severely handicapped by the tradition that it was a 'second-best', an alternative to be considered only when hope of a place in a Grammar school had gone. This handicap was perpetuated, and indeed, aggravated by the fact that for years after 1944 many, if not most, Secondary Technical schools continued to receive their entrants at twelve or thirteen instead of, as did the other Secondary schools, at eleven-plus.

Thirdly, in many cases Secondary Technical schools did not for years have their own separate buildings; they were housed in Technical Colleges, using accommodation, and often equipment, primarily intended for adult students. Not infrequently some of their teachers were principally concerned with adult students, and taught in the Secondary Technical school in order to make up a full week's programme.

Despite these handicaps many Secondary Technical schools built up fine reputations, though only rarely did they manage to recruit a body of pupils of equal intellectual calibre with the Grammar school. They were always supported by a loyal, if small, body of opinion which believed them to be uniquely valuable. During the 1960s they tended increasingly to offer courses similar to those in Grammar schools – with, generally, rather more time given to woodwork, metalwork, measured drawing, workshop and/or studio activities, and rather less to the humanities. They also entered pupils for the GCE at both Ordinary and Advanced levels. This assimilation of curricula led to a number of amalgamations, usually bilateral Grammar-Technicals.

Secondary Modern Schools

The development of the Secondary Modern school during the 1950s and the early 1960s was extremely diverse. When, in 1945, the Senior Elementary schools were, by a stroke of the pen, transformed into Secondary Modern schools, the expectation (at least of the Ministry of Education) was that they would "provide a good all-round secondary education, not focused primarily on the traditional subjects of the school curriculum, but developing out of the interests of the children".[14] They were to be "free from the pressure of external examinations",[15] and their teachers were encouraged to experiment in order to discover the most appropriate forms of education for the children in their charge.

The twenty years following 1945 saw in many Secondary Modern schools a process of evolution unmatched for speed and significance in the history of English education. Some account of the earlier years of this evolution I endeavoured to present in 1958,[16] and other authors have dealt with various aspects of it. But the full story remains to be told; when it is, it will prove to be as exciting and encouraging a story as any to be found in the annals of education. A dominant cause was the readiness with which numerous teachers seized the opportunity offered them to experiment. In particular, they devised a wide variety of 'special'[17] courses, most of them with a vocational or semi-vocational bias. An investigation made in 1956 by the National Union of Teachers covering seventy-eight of the 146 LEA areas showed that nearly fifty of these authorities had organized schemes for the development of such courses. The courses included:

Art and Crafts; Catering; Homecraft; Needlework and Design; Automobile Engineering; Mechanical Trades; House Maintenance and Furnishing; Practical Crafts; Craftsmanship; Rural Science; Farming and Gardening; Music; Seamanship; General Science; Electrical Science; Commercial Subjects; Nursing; Academic subjects for GCE. The last was the largest group of all.

Such courses led to a rapid increase in the number of pupils staying on at school 'beyond compulsory school age'. Among the 'special' courses the one which made the most spectacular advance – and caused the greatest controversy – was the academic course leading to the GCE. In 1954 (only three years after the GCE was introduced) 357 Secondary Modern schools presented about 5,500 candidates for examination; ten years later the number of schools had increased five-fold, and of candidates ten-fold. By comparison with the Grammar school, the number of Modern school candidates was small; most aimed at Ordinary Level passes only, and averaged an entry of only four subjects a candidate. The pass ratio – just over half – was also somewhat lower than that of the Grammar school. Nevertheless, it was an amazing – and completely unanticipated – achievement for a group of schools supposed originally to cater for 'non-academic' children only.

And the GCE was far from being the only external examination which Secondary Modern school pupils were taking. Considerable numbers were entered for the examinations of the Royal Society of Arts, the College of Preceptors, and various regional bodies: the Union of Lancashire and Cheshire Institutes, the Northern Counties Technical Examinations Council, the East Midlands Educational Union, and the Union of Educational Institutions. Some boys' schools entered candidates for the examinations leading to admission into apprenticeships in HM Dockyards and the Armed Forces. Examinations conducted by commercial organizations, such as Pitman, and voluntary associations – for example, the British Red Cross – also attracted candidates. Finally, a number of LEAs began to organize their own local 'Leaving Certificates'. The examinations for these were usually taken at the end of the candidates' fourth year in the Secondary Modern school, and the level of attainment required was such as could be achieved by the top 30 to 50 per cent of pupils.

In 1963, following a report by a sub-committee of the Secondary School Examinations Council (SSEC) on "Secondary School Examinations other than the GCE" (the 'Beloe' Report), the Minister of Education announced that he had approved the introduction of a new, officially recognized, external examination for a 'Certificate of Secondary Education' (CSE). This examination, designed to overlap with 'O' level GCE at one end, and to cater for pupils of slightly below average ability at the other, could be taken (voluntarily) by pupils in any type of school who had completed – or almost completed – five years of secondary education, but was intended especially for Secondary Modern schools. Like the GCE, it would be on a subject basis, that is, success in a single subject would secure a Certificate. Most importantly, the examination was to be controlled by teachers serving in the schools providing the candidates. During 1963–64 fourteen Regional Boards were established to administer the CSE, and nine of these conducted their first examinations in the summer of 1965. All were in operation in 1966. An original feature of the CSE examinations was that there would be no failures; candidates would be placed in one of five grades, of which Grade I represented a standard equivalent to 'O' level GCE. To obtain a Certificate, however, a candidate had to obtain at least a Grade IV pass in one subject.

It must not be assumed from the foregoing that all, or even most, Secondary Modern schools became obsessed with external examinations. Many teachers were strongly opposed to introducing them. But over the years they tended to decrease in number. For a variety of reasons – including a burning desire to prove to the public that the Secondary Modern school was definitely not a school for 'failures' – an increasing number of teachers turned to external examinations to justify their belief that the intellectual ability of their pupils was far higher than was generally believed, and to give children the opportunities their abilities merited.

By the late 1950s one could no longer talk about *the* Secondary Modern school; one could only think in terms of a number of different types of Secondary Modern schools. In my *Interim Report* I attempted to analyse the situation as I saw it in the school year 1956–57. Then I distinguished four main groups of schools: (1) those giving little more than the old Senior Elementary school curriculum – and therefore not really providing secondary education; (2) those giving a sound training in the basic subjects, and opportunities for advanced work in one or more subjects or activities; (3) those giving a general curriculum, without specializing in any branch but frequently allotting a greater proportion of time to art and crafts, and to social and aesthetic activities, than the Grammar school; and (4) those giving a general curriculum during the first two or three years and a choice of 'special' courses thereafter. There were many variants of these stereotypes, such as, for example, the rural school with a strong agricultural or horticultural bias throughout, and the town school with a similarly dominant technical or commercial bias.

Those groupings were still distinguishable ten years later, but greatly altered in size. The first, unfortunately, had not been altogether eliminated. The fourth had grown largely, but its 'special courses' had tended in many cases to become one course only, an academic course leading to GCE and/or CSE. Many Secondary Modern schools providing a variety of courses had, however, been merged in Comprehensive schools or had themselves been designated Comprehensive.

Comprehensive Schools

The Comprehensive school has been a storm centre of controversy ever since the idea was mooted in the 1920s. Yet in respect of curriculum (or, frequently, pupil numbers) there was during the 1950s and 1960s little to distinguish some Comprehensive schools from some Bilaterals (there were instances of schools which changed their titles more than once), or even from large Secondary Modern schools offering five or six 'special' courses. As the number of Comprehensives grew, however, it became clear that the large 'all through' school was adding new and distinctive elements to English secondary education. Its great range of ability and aptitudes was compelling a rethinking of the organizational and pastoral functions of the Head, the Departmental heads, and the assistant staff. Academically, one of the most valuable developments has been the increased and skilful attention paid to children with learning difficulties.

One important development (not confined to Comprehensive schools) was the spread of 'resource centres', providing:

> a central store for books, non-book printed material, audio-visual equipment and the software to use with it, including slides, filmstrips, films, film-loops and film cassettes, microforms, phono-recordings and video-recordings, models and specimens.[18]

The early 1970s saw the revival of the 'Community College', first brilliantly initiated in the 1920s and 1930s by Henry Morris, then secretary for education in Cambridgeshire. Current conceptions of a Community College, or Centre, are even more ambitious than Morris's. The Abraham Moss Centre at Manchester, for example, includes:

an eight-form entry comprehensive school; a college of further education; an adult education centre; a shared-use district sports centre and district library; a crèche adjoining the children's library; a performing arts centre including theatre, drama studio and music suite; a youth wing that will double as a students' union facility during the day; an aged and handicapped people's club; and a small residential wing that will house up to thirteen staff and students.[19]

References

1 *Secondary Education, with Special Reference to Grammar Schools and Technical High Schools.* HMSO, 1938.
2 *Curriculum and Examinations in Secondary Schools.* HMSO, 1943.
3 *Educational Reconstruction.* HMSO, 1943. p. 10.
4 'All-age' schools, though containing senior pupils, were officially designated Primary.
5 'Spens' Report, pp. xix–xxii.
6 *Secondary School Selection.* A British Psychological Society Inquiry. Edited by P. E. Vernon, Methuen, 1957.
7 Circular 10/65, dated 12 July 1965.
8 Circular 10/70, dated 30 June 1970.
9 Circular 4/74, dated 16 April 1974.
10 Circular 144, dated 16 June 1947.
11 *The New Secondary Education.* Ministry of Education Pamphlet No. 9. HMSO, 1947. p. 25.
12 *The Schools Regulations 1959* (SI 1959, No. 364), Regulation 15.
13 *The New Secondary Education*, pp. 47 and 48.
14 ibid, p. 29.
15 *The Nation's Schools.* Ministry of Education Pamphlet No. 1. HMSO, 1945, p. 21.
16 *Secondary Modern Schools*: An Interim Report. Routledge & Kegan Paul, 1958.
17 These courses were called by a variety of names: 'special', 'biased', 'advanced', 'extended' were among the commonest.
18 *Education* Digest, 18 October 1974.
19 *Education*, 21 February 1975. Article by Jackson Hall, Deputy Education Officer, Manchester.

Further reading

BENN, C., and SIMON, B., *Half Way There*: Report on the British comprehensive school reform. Penguin, 2nd edition, 1972.

BESWICK, NORMAN, *Organizing Resources: Six Case Studies*; The Final Report of the Schools Council Resource Centre Project. Heinemann, 1975.

DEMPSTER, J. J. B., *Purpose in the Modern School*. Methuen, 1956.

DENT, H. C., *Secondary Modern Schools, An Interim Report*. Routledge & Kegan Paul, 1958.

EDWARDS, REESE, *The Secondary Technical School*. University of London Press Ltd, 1960.

Inner London Education Authority, *London Comprehensive Schools 1966*. ILEA, 1967.

JACKSON, BRIAN, and MARSDEN, DENNIS, *Education and the Working Class*. Routledge & Kegan Paul, 1962; Penguin, 1966.

KNEEBONE, R. M. T., *I Work in a Secondary Modern School*. Routledge & Kegan Paul, 1957.

MASON, S. C., *The Leicestershire Experiment and Plan*. Councils and Education Press, 3rd (revised) edition, 1963.

MONKS, T. G., *Comprehensive Education in England and Wales*. National Foundation for Educational Research, 1968.

MONTGOMERY, R. J., *Examinations*: An Account of their evolution as administrative devices in England. Longmans, 1965.

RÉE, H. A., *The Essential Grammar School*. Harrap, 1956.

RUBENSTEIN, DAVID, and SIMON, BRIAN, *The Evolution of the Comprehensive School 1926–1966*. Routledge & Kegan Paul, 2nd edition, 1973.

STEVENS, FRANCES, *The Living Tradition. The social and educational assumptions of the grammar school*. Hutchinson, 3rd edition, 1972.

TAYLOR, P. H., REID, W. A., and HOLLEY, B. J., *The English Sixth Form*. Routledge & Kegan Paul, 1974. *The Sixth Form College in Practice*: A Symposium by Education Officers in seven LEAs. Councils and Education Press, 1973.

TAYLOR, WILLIAM, *The Secondary Modern School*. Faber, 1963.

VERNON, P. E. (ed.), *Secondary School Selection*. Methuen, 1957.

WISEMAN, S. (ed.), *Examinations and English Education*. Manchester University Press, 1962.

YATES, A., and PIDGEON, D. A., *Admission to Grammar Schools*. Newnes, 1957.

Official

Ministry of Education Annual Report for 1951, pp. 11–12 (note on the 11+).

Secondary Education with Special Reference to Grammar Schools and Technical High Schools ('Spens' Report) 1938.

Curriculum and Examinations in Secondary Schools ('Norwood' Report), 1943.

The New Secondary Education Ministry of Education (Pamphlet 9), 1947.

Examinations in Secondary Schools (Report of the Secondary School Examinations Council), 1947.

15 to 18 ('Crowther' Report). Report of the Central Advisory Council for Education (England). Vol. I, Report, 1959, Vol II, Surveys, 1960.

Secondary School Examinations other than the G.C.E. ('Beloe' Report), 1960.

The Certificate of Secondary Education. (Report of the Secondary School Examinations Council), 1962.

Half Our Future ('Newsom' Report). Report of the Central Advisory Council for Education (England), 1963.

All from H.M. Stationery Office.

Department of Education and Science Report on Education No. 87. *The Growth of Comprehensive Education*. March 1977. Free from Information Division, Room 1/27, DES, Elizabeth House, York Road, London SE1 7PH.

CHAPTER 6 | # Education of Handicapped Children

Section 8(2) (c) of the Education Act 1944 requires LEAs, in fulfilment of their duty to provide sufficient schools, to have particular regard to:

the need for securing that provision is made for pupils who suffer from any disability of mind or body by providing, either in special schools or otherwise, special educational treatment, that is to say, education by special methods appropriate for persons suffering from that disability.

Section 34(1) makes it the statutory duty of the LEA "to ascertain what children in their area require special educational treatment", and lays down that:

for the purpose of fulfilling that duty any officer of a local education authority authorized in that behalf by the authority may by notice in writing served upon the parent of any child who has attained the age of two years require him to submit the child for examination by a medical officer of the authority for advice as to whether the child is suffering from any disability of mind or body, and as to the nature and extent of any such disability. . . .

Failure by the parent (without reasonable excuse) to comply with this requirement renders him liable "on summary conviction to a fine not exceeding five pounds". On the other hand Section 34(2) says that:

If the parent of any child who has attained the age of two requests the local education authority for the area to cause the child to be so medically examined as aforesaid, the authority shall comply with the request unless in their opinion the request is unreasonable.

The National Health Service Reorganisation Act 1973 transferred, as from 1 April 1974, the School Health Service from the LEAs to Area Health Authorities (AHAs) working under the direction of the Secretary of State for Health and Social Security, and responsible for the National Health Service as a whole. This Act did not, however, remove from LEAs the responsibility to ascertain handicapped children, and to ensure that they received special educational treatment. LEAS continue also to be responsible for the provision of premises for Special schools. AHAs are responsible for ensuring that medical and any other necessary health service staff are available to LEAs to enable them to fulfil these responsibilities. There are joint AHA-LEA committees for consultation and planning.

The provisions of the 1944 Act represented a very great advance on previous legislation. The LEAs' duty of ascertainment had hitherto been confined to "children who by reason of mental or physical defect are incapable of receiving proper benefit from the instruction in the ordinary public elementary schools", and to children "unfit by reason of severe epilepsy to attend the public elementary schools".[1] Moreover, this duty applied only to children aged five and over. The duty to make special provision covered only five groups of children – blind, deaf, physically handicapped, mentally defective, and epileptic.[2] Like the duty of ascertainment, it was limited to children of five years old and upwards who were attending, or expected to attend, the Public Elementary school; and it was restricted to the provision of special schools for such children.

Further beneficial changes made by the 1944 Act were that the age of entry into compulsory education was made the same for handicapped children as for normal children[3] (previously it had been seven except for blind and deaf children), and that a child had no longer to be certified as mentally or physically defective before he could be provided with education appropriate to his particular needs. The omission of the latter requirement was especially happy, because having a child certified as mentally defective, and consequently segregated from his fellows in a Special school – the 'looney' school as it was often called – had been a cause of deep humiliation to numerous parents. Since 1944 handicapped children have no longer been regarded as a class apart: the provision for them of 'special educational treatment' is part of the general duty laid upon the LEAs to provide educational facilities for school children suitable to their ages, abilities and aptitudes.

In order to ensure that every handicapped child shall receive appropriate 'special educational treatment', Section 33(1) of the 1944 Act requires the Minister to make Regulations:

> defining the several categories of pupils requiring special educational treatment and making provision as to the special methods appropriate for the education of pupils of each category.

The categories thus defined[4] are:

(a) *Blind Pupils.* Pupils who have no sight or whose sight is or is likely to become so defective that they require education by methods not involving the use of sight.

(b) *Partially Sighted Pupils.* Pupils who by reason of defective vision cannot follow the normal régime of ordinary schools without detriment to their sight or to their educational development, but can be educated by special methods involving the use of sight.

(c) *Deaf Pupils.* Pupils who have no hearing or whose hearing is so defective that they require education by methods used for deaf pupils without naturally acquired speech or language.

(d) *Partially Hearing Pupils.* Pupils who have some naturally acquired speech and language but whose hearing is so defective that they require for their education special arrangements or facilities though not necessarily all the educational methods used for deaf pupils.

(*e*) *Educationally Sub-Normal Pupils.* Pupils who, by reason of limited ability, or other conditions resulting in educational retardation, require some specialized form of education wholly or partly in substitution for the education normally given in ordinary schools.

(*f*) *Epileptic Pupils.* Pupils who by reason of epilepsy cannot be educated under the normal régime of ordinary schools without detriment to themselves or other pupils.

(*g*) *Maladjusted Pupils.* Pupils who show evidence of emotional instability or psychological disturbance and require special educational treatment in order to effect their personal, social, or educational readjustment.

(*h*) *Physically Handicapped Pupils.* Pupils not suffering solely from a defect of sight or hearing who by reason of disease or crippling defect cannot, without detriment to their health or educational development, be satisfactorily educated under the normal régime of ordinary schools.

(*i*) *Pupils Suffering from Speech Defect.* Pupils who on account of defect or lack of speech not due to deafness require special educational treatment.

(*j*) *Delicate Pupils.* Pupils not in any other category who by reason of impaired physical condition need a change of environment or cannot, without risk to their health or educational development, be educated under the normal régime of ordinary schools.

It is the national policy that handicapped children shall be educated in ordinary schools unless their disability renders this impracticable, or undesirable – the latter either in their own interests or those of their school fellows. So far as possible, handicapped children are to be educated along with ordinary children, so that they may participate in the normal life of society.[5]

In recent years opposition has grown to the idea of fixed categories.[6] But up to the end of 1976 these had not been abolished.

Special educational treatment was in 1976 being provided in:

(*a*) Ordinary schools.
(*b*) Special schools, day or boarding.
(*c*) Special schools in hospitals, and
(*d*) Individually to children in hospital or at home.

Just as it is national policy that, wherever practicable, a handicapped pupil shall be educated in an ordinary school, so it is also policy that "Where a Special school is necessary, a day school is preferable if it offers a satisfactory and practicable solution"; that is to say, whenever possible handicapped children are not to be deprived of home life. Boarding Special schools and boarding Homes for handicapped pupils are to be "reserved for those cases where there is no satisfactory alternative solution".[7]

Until 1973 the maximum number of children permitted in Special school classes was smaller than the number permitted in the ordinary Primary school. The maxima were:

Children who are deaf, partially hearing, or
    suffering from speech defect   10
Blind, partially sighted, or maladjusted   15
Educationally subnormal, epileptic, or physically
    handicapped   20
Delicate   30

In 1973 the more flexible medium of staff–pupil ratios was substituted. This has the great advantage that it permits the size of classes to be varied according to the activities being pursued.[8]

The provisions of the Education Act 1944 relating to handicapped children were designed to "open the way to fuller and better provision for children handicapped by physical or mental disabilities".[9] They have, happily, very largely realized the hopes which inspired them. One well-informed commentator declared in 1958 that:

In 1944 probably no one thought that the section of the community which, regarded as a section, would profit most from the new Education Act would be children with physical or mental handicaps, but such has in fact been the case.[10]

In the years between 1944 and 1971 (when the inclusion of the severely sub-normal children took place) the number of Special schools was doubled. And the quality of the new accommodation was often incomparably better than the old – though much of the latter had been greatly improved by reconstruction, redecoration and re-equipment.

Special schools are provided by LEAs, voluntary bodies, and hospitals. Much the greatest number is provided by the LEAs.

Thanks to the large additional provision of Special schools since 1944 the number of places available for most categories of handicapped children was by the late 1960s sufficient, or almost so. For one or two categories, indeed, the accommodation had had to be reduced. But there was still a severe shortage of places for educationally sub-normal (ESN) children, and many more places were wanted for the maladjusted. The ESN category, always by far the largest, has always had much the longest waiting list, despite the fact that over the years the provision of additional accommodation for ESN children has far exceeded in quantity that made for all the other categories together. An inquiry made by the Ministry in 1956 suggested that the number of ESN children in ordinary schools who ought really to have been in Special schools was more than twice as large as the waiting list. There is little doubt about the reason for this; Medical Officers of Health, well aware of the grave deficiency of accommodation, had in previous years refrained from recommending for entry into Special schools all but severe cases of educational subnormality. As the number of places available increased, so the MOs made recommendations more freely, with the result that in some years the waiting list actually increased in size. The next longest waiting list, that of maladjusted children, is ordinarily about one-fifth as large.

Concurrently with the expansion and improvement of accommodation great advances have been made in the education and training of handicapped children, and in diagnosing and treating their ills. One very important development was the distinction drawn between blind and partially-sighted children. Very many of the latter can now receive their education in ordinary schools. But not all; there are about a dozen day Special schools for partially-sighted children, and a boarding school, Exhall Grange near Coventry, which was established in 1951 by the Warwickshire LEA.

No greater advances have been made in any field of special educational treatment than in that of the education of the deaf and the partially hearing. This is very largely due to the brilliant research and experimental work which has been done for many years by the Manchester University Department of Audiology and Education of the Deaf, founded in 1919 by Sir James Jones in memory of his son, who was born deaf, and directed for a quarter of a century by Dr Irene Ewing. Two of the most important discoveries made in this department are that deafness can be ascertained in children only a few weeks old, and that it is possible to begin to train them to understand speech before they are twelve months old. As a result, very many more young children than previously are now to be found in Special schools for the deaf. Parents are shown how to give their children training at home during infancy, and the children pass on to a Special school at the age of two or shortly after. Thanks to progressively refined diagnostic techniques, it has also become increasingly possible to distinguish early between totally deaf children and those with some hearing capacity.

In 1949 the Berkshire LEA opened Donnington Lodge, near Newbury, the first residential Nursery school for deaf children to be maintained by an LEA. There are boarding schools for deaf children between the ages of seven and twelve at Basingstoke in Hampshire and Caterham in Surrey. For intellectually able children of Secondary school age there are the Mary Hare Grammar School for the Deaf at Newbury in Berkshire, a co-educational school, and Burwood Park School in Surrey, which provides education with a technical bias for boys. In 1964 the London County Council began providing full-time courses of Further education for students who had recently left Special schools for the deaf; in 1974 its successor, the Inner London Education Authority, was providing similar facilities at the City Literary Institute and the Brixton College of Further Education. Courses were also available in Birmingham, Manchester, and Worksop.

The term 'physically handicapped' covers a widely various and constantly changing group, of which the most characteristic feature is lack of ability in moving. Improvement in medical treatment, especially preventive treatment, is steadily reducing the number of physically handicapped children who must be educated in Special schools. There has been, however, since the late 1950s an increase in the number of children surviving with *spina bifida*, for which there is no known cure. Other diseases commonly found include cerebral palsy, congenital heart disease, and muscular dystrophy.

Very great public attention has been given since 1944 to children (commonly

A class of deaf children in a special school

called 'spastics') who suffer from cerebral palsy, and greatly improved methods of dealing with them have been developed, though unhappily no means of preventing the disability have been discovered. In 1947 St. Margaret's School, Croydon, was opened as the first boarding Special school exclusively for spastic children; it was followed in 1948 by Carlson House, Birmingham, the first day-school solely for spastics. In 1959 the first school buildings designed specially for spastic children were opened at Ivybridge, Devon, to be followed in 1961 by Ingfield Manor at Billingshurst in Sussex for children of low intelligence. There are also many boarding Special schools which accept spastics along with children who are physically handicapped in other ways. Lightly affected spastic children can be educated in ordinary schools. In 1963 the Spastics Society opened Dene Park near Tonbridge in Kent as a Further education centre for 16- and 17-year-old school-leavers suffering from severe physical handicap, and in 1964 donated £600,000, to be spread over ten years, to the University of London Institute of Education for research on child development, including the special problems of spastic children, and for the training of teachers of handicapped children. In 1967 the Society opened Meldreth Training School near Royston in Cambridgeshire, the first residential training unit in the country for severely sub-normal spastic children.

The medical treatment of epileptics has been greatly improved since 1944.

Anti-convulsant drugs enable many children who formerly would have been sent to Special schools to attend ordinary schools. This puts an added responsibility on their teachers, because in spite of the control effected by the drugs these children nevertheless need special care. Frequent attacks can impair intelligence, and heavy dosing can slow down reactions.

Delicate children remain one of the larger groups, but their numbers are decreasing, and the character of the complaints from which they suffer is changing. There are now few cases of malnutrition, and few of tuberculosis, formerly a widespread and deadly scourge of childhood. Among the chief ailments in the 1970s were asthma, bronchitis, diabetes, obesity, mild or moderate emotional disturbance, and debility after severe illness. Many children classified as delicate, however, had also some physical defect.

The category of maladjusted children dates from 1945. The number in it is considerable, but about half of the children deemed maladjusted remain in attendance at ordinary schools, and receive treatment in child guidance clinics, mainly provided by LEAs. In 1955 a committee set up by the Minister of Education (the 'Underwood' committee) reviewed the various methods used in treating maladjusted children, and laid down the general principle that:

a maladjusted child, whenever possible, should continue to live at home during treatment and attend an ordinary school; that where a child requires to attend a special school or class, it is preferable that he should continue to live at home while doing so unless it is unlikely that he can be successfully treated while he stays at home; and that, where it is necessary to treat a child away from home, the objective should be to prepare the way for his return at the earliest possible date.[11]

In order that treatment should be everywhere available the Committee recommended that:

there should be a comprehensive child guidance service available for the area of every local education authority, involving a school psychological service, the School Health Service and Child Guidance Clinic(s), all of which should work in close co-operation[12]

The Ministers of Education and Health both accepted this recommendation, and urged LEAs and regional hospital boards to plan jointly the development of the child guidance service.

In the early 1960s considerable public attention began to be given to psychotic children with 'autistic' symptoms, that is, children who, though without obvious sensory or mental defects, are, because of severe emotional disturbance, unable to communicate or form normal relationships with other people. In 1962 the National Society for Autistic Children was formed; in 1965 it opened its first school, at Ealing. In 1964 a national conference was held to survey existing provision for such children and to plan future policy. In 1966 the DES and the Calouste Gulbenkian Foundation jointly financed a three-year research project, at the University of London Institute of Psychiatry, designed to assess the value of different kinds of special educational treatment given to autistic children.

The category of children suffering from speech defects also dates from 1945, though (as with maladjusted children) children were being given help with speech difficulties by some LEAs before the war. A grave shortage of speech therapists had, however, held up the spread of treatment. In 1945, when treatment for speech defects was imposed as a duty on LEAs, the two professional organizations training speech therapists combined to form the College of Speech Therapists. Within ten years the number of speech therapists employed by LEAs had increased fivefold, from 70 to 350. During the same period the number of children referred for treatment increased in as great a proportion; in 1955 it was 44,840. Few children have to be sent to Special schools solely on account of speech defect, but in 1947 Moor House School was established at Oxted in Surrey to deal with severe cases. This school, which was enlarged in 1961, has done pioneer work on the causes and treatment of speech disorders.

Consideration of the educationally sub-normal has been deferred to the last because this category – swollen in 1971 by the addition of some 35,000 severely sub-normal (ESN/S) children – has always been by far the largest. Mention has been made of the fact that there is what appears to be a permanent waiting list (of great length) of children for places in ESN Special schools; and this despite the fact that a larger increase in the number of places provided has been made than for any other category. What is encouraging in an otherwise depressing situation is the revolutionary change in attitude towards ESN children which has taken place since 1944. Previously, they were regarded (and officially described) as 'mental defectives', and classed in people's minds with lunatics. Today they are recognized as a relatively large group (from 5 to 10 per cent) of the school population which requires special educational treatment, but which given this will, most of them, grow up into useful and acceptable members of society.

In 1968 the Government announced that responsibility for the education of severely sub-normal children was to be transferred from the DHSS to the DES. This transfer was effected by the Education (Handicapped Children) Act 1970, the takeover date being 1 April 1971. Of the 35,000 children transferred, about 27,000 were receiving some form of education, in 425 Junior Training Centres (JTCs) administered by the local Health authorities. The other 8,000 were in hospitals for the mentally handicapped; about half of them attended schools on the premises, but the other half received no formal education. The significance of the transfer was that all ESN/S children became entitled to education in school; they were no longer to be regarded as 'ineducable' (as they had been officially until 1959), or even as 'unsuitable for education at school' – the euphemism used between 1959 and 1971.

Many JTCs and hospitals were inadequately staffed and equipped for formal education. The LEAs in most cases quickly transformed the lot of the JTC teacher by supplying more staff and equipment, as a prelude to turning the JTCs into Special schools. The latter job had not been completed by 1976, and the plight of ESN/S children in some hospitals was still far from satisfactory.

Training of Teachers

For teaching blind, deaf, and partially-hearing children in Special schools teachers must have specialist qualifications in addition to the qualifications entitling them to the status of Qualified Teacher. For teaching children in all other categories, whether in a Special or an ordinary school, specialist qualifications are not obligatory, although as long ago as 1954 the NACTST recommended in its Fourth Report that:

> teachers wishing to enter special schools should, after experience in ordinary schools, and after some preliminary experience with handicapped children, take a full-time course of additional training.

The supply and training of specialist teachers qualified to give special educational treatment to handicapped children (other than the blind and the deaf) long remained less than satisfactory. In the 1960s the position improved. The Department of Child Development in the University of London Institute of Education was greatly enlarged, thanks to the generous grant from the Spastics Society, and by 1970 was running Diploma courses for teachers of ESN, maladjusted, physically handicapped, deaf and partially-hearing children. Some thirty other Institutes, Colleges and Departments of Education were also offering one-year courses for teachers of handicapped children.

Of the 3,000 teachers of ESN/S children who were transferred from the DHSS to LEA service in April 1971 about 1,000 held the Diploma of the Training Council for Teachers of Mentally Handicapped Children. This had involved a two-year course for school-leavers, or a one-year course for experienced persons over the age of 24. The DES granted Qualified Teacher status to holders of this Diploma who had five or more years' experience of teaching ESN/S children, and offered one-year full-time 'conversion' courses to the others. This offer ended in 1972; from then all prospective teachers of ESN/S children have had to take a three-year course.

In 1974 the Secretary of State for Education and Science appointed a Committee of Enquiry, under the chairmanship of Mrs Mary Warnock, a Research Fellow in Philosophy at Lady Margaret Hall, Oxford, with the following terms of reference:

> To review educational provision in England, Scotland and Wales for children and young people handicapped by disabilities of body or mind, taking account of the medical aspects of their needs, together with arrangements to prepare them for entry into employment; to consider the most effective use of resources for these purposes; and to make recommendations.

This committee was still pursuing its investigation at the end of 1976.

References

1 Education Act 1921, Section 55(1).
2 ibid, Section 62.
3 By the wording of sections 35 and 36 in the Education Act 1944.
4 See *The Handicapped Pupils and Special Schools Regulations 1959* (SI 1959, No. 365), Part II.
5 See Section 33(2) of the Education Act 1944, and Circular 276, *Provision of Special Schools*, dated 25 June 1954.
6 See DES Report No. 77, *Special Education: A Fresh Look*, issued April 1973.
7 Circular 276.
8 See Circular 4/73.
9 *Explanatory Memorandum to the Education Bill*, 1943.
10 Peter Quince, in *The Schoolmaster*, 10 January 1958.
11 Quoted from Circular 348, *Special Educational Treatment for Maladjusted Children*, dated 10 March 1959. This Circular contains the Minister's comments on parts of the Underwood report.
12 Quoted from Circular 347, *Child Guidance*, dated 10 March 1959. This Circular contains the Minister's comments on that part of the Underwood report dealing with child guidance.

Further reading

AXFORD, W. A., *Handicapped Children in Britain: their problems and education: books and articles published in Great Britain from the 1944 Education Act to 1958*. Library Association, 1959.

BURN, MICHAEL, *Mr. Lyward's Answer*. Hamilton, 1956.

BURT, CYRIL, *The Backward Child*. University of London Press Ltd, 5th edition, 1961.

CLEUGH, M. F. (ed.), *Teaching the Slow Learner*. Methuen, 1961.

EWING, I. R. and A. W. G., *New Opportunities for deaf children*. University of London Press Ltd, 1958.

HERMELIN, B. and O'CONNOR, N., *Psychological Experiments with Autistic Children*. Pergamon, 1970.

HEWETT, SHEILA (with JOHN and ELISABETH NEWSON), *The Family and the Handicapped Child*. Allen & Unwin, 1970.

JACKSON, S., *Special Education in England and Wales*. Oxford University Press, 1966.

JOHNSON, J. C., *Educating Hearing-impaired Children in Ordinary Schools*. Manchester University Press, 1962.

KERSHAW, J. D., *Handicapped Children*. Heinemann, 1961.

LEWIS, M. M., *Language and Personality in Deaf Children*. National Foundation for Educational Research in England and Wales, 1968.

LOWENFELD, BERTHOLD (ed.), *The Visually handicapped child in school*. Constable, 1974.

PRITCHARD, D. G., *Education of the Handicapped 1760–1960*. Routledge & Kegan Paul, 1963.

SEGAL, S. S., *No Child is Ineducable*. Special Education – Provisions and Trends. Pergamon Press, 1967.

Official

Ministry of Education Annual Reports, and biennial reports on *The Health of the School Child.*

Special Educational Treatment (Pamphlet 5), 1946.

Training and Supply of Teachers of Handicapped Pupils. (Fourth Report of the NACTST), 1954.

Education of the Handicapped Pupil 1945–55 (Pamphlet 30, reprinted from the Ministry's Annual Report for 1955).

Report of the Committee on Maladjusted Children (the 'Underwood' Report), 1955.

The Education of Maladjusted Children (Pamphlet 47), 1965.

Blind and Partially Sighted Children. Education Survey No. 4, 1968.

Peripatetic Teachers of the Deaf. Education Survey No. 6, 1969.

Circular 15/70. *The Education (Handicapped Children) Act 1970. Responsibility for the Education of Mentally Handicapped Children.* September 1970.

All the above from H.M. Stationery Office.

Department of Education and Science Report on Education No. 77, *Special Education: A Fresh Look*, April 1973. Free from Information Division, DES.

CHAPTER 7 | # Welfare Services

The principal welfare services available to schoolchildren are the Children's Health Service and the School Milk and Meals Services. All were preceded by voluntary provision, but Health and Meals Services were incorporated into the statutory system of public education as early as the first decade of the present century.

A School Medical Service was established by the Education (Administrative Provisions) Act 1907. This made it a duty of LEAs to provide free medical examination of all children attending Public Elementary schools, and gave them power to make arrangements for attending to the health and physical condition of these children. The arrangements had to be approved by the Board of Education, which established a Medical Branch to supervise and co-ordinate them. The Branch was extremely fortunate in its first head, Dr G. (later Sir George) Newman, who made it from the start an effective weapon against the then widespread disease and defect among Elementary school pupils.

Subsequent Acts enabled LEAs to provide various forms of medical (including dental) treatment; and Regulations made under the Education Act 1918 required them to provide treatment for "minor ailments, defective vision, dental disease, enlarged tonsils, and adenoids". Such treatment had to be paid for by parents, except in cases of attested poverty.

The Education Act 1944 extended the duty of medical inspection to cover also maintained Secondary schools and compulsory part-time Further education, and of treatment to cover all forms of preventive and regulatory treatment, and made the provision of treatment, like inspection, free. Section 48 required every LEA:

> to provide for the medical inspection, at appropriate intervals, of pupils in attendance at any school or county college maintained by them.

and

> to make such arrangements for securing the provision of free medical treatment for pupils in attendance at any school or county college maintained by them as are necessary for securing that comprehensive facilities for free medical treatment are available to them either under this Act or otherwise.

Section 78(2) of the 1944 Act empowered LEAs to make arrangements with the proprietors of independent schools to provide for the medical inspection and treatment of the pupils in their schools. "So far as is practicable," the expense incurred by the LEA was not to exceed per head that incurred on children in maintained schools.

Regulations made under the Act required every LEA to maintain a School Health Service (the title 'Medical' was dropped), and, as part of that Service, a School Dental Service. Each LEA had to appoint a Principal School Medical Officer and a Principal School Dental Officer; and such other medical and dental officers, nurses, dental technicians, and other persons as were needed to make the Service efficient.

The National Health Service Act 1946, which came into operation in 1948, empowered LEAs to make arrangements with Regional Hospital Boards and teaching hospitals for free specialist and hospital treatment for children attending maintained schools.

Until 1959 the School Health Service Regulations required LEAs to see that every pupil had a general medical inspection on not fewer than three occasions during the period of compulsory school age (five to fifteen), and a dental inspection as soon as possible after first entering school. From 1959 these arrangements were left to the discretion of the LEAs, who had still, however, to keep medical and dental records, in a form approved by the Minister, for all pupils in maintained schools. Parents had to be given the opportunity, "so far as is reasonable and practicable", to be present at every medical inspection of their child/children, and at the first dental inspection. From 1959, in accordance with a suggestion made the previous year by the Chief Medical Officer of the Ministry of Education in his biennial Report,[1] an increasing number of school doctors did fewer routine checks, in order to spend more time on 'selective' inspection, that is, inspection of children with known defects.

Under the National Health Service Reorganization Act 1973 the School Health Service was integrated in a reconstituted National Health Service controlled and directed by the DHSS, and administered locally by Area Health Authorities (AHAs) whose areas were co-terminous with those of the LEAs established by the Local Government Act 1972. (In the Greater London area, which was untouched by the 1972 Act, the AHAs operate within the boundaries of a borough or combination of boroughs.) The LEAs, however, retained responsibility for the ascertainment of children in need of special educational treatment, and for the provision of Special schools; it is the statutory duty of the AHA to ensure that the necessary Health Service staff are available to the LEA for these purposes.

School Meals Service

Like the School Health Service, the statutory School Meals Service was preceded by voluntary provision. But whereas many LEAs had begun to play quite a large part in the provision of medical services before the Act of 1907 made it their statutory duty (forty-eight had a system of medical inspection by 1905, and eighty-five employed school medical officers), few did anything about school meals before the Education (Provision of Meals) Act 1906. Practically all the meals provided for school children were provided by voluntary bodies.

The differing attitudes towards these services were reflected in the legislation enacted before 1944. The Education (Administrative Provisions) Act 1907 laid upon the LEAs a statutory duty to provide a medical service, but the Education (Provision of Meals) Act 1906 imposed no such duty. It merely gave the authorities permissive powers to assist voluntary effort or themselves to provide meals for "children attending an elementary school within their area . . . unable by reason of lack of food to take advantage of the education provided for them".

Moreover, until 1914 the expenditure which might be incurred by LEAs on school meals was limited to the product of a halfpenny rate (ie, under ¼p); and the meals could be provided only on days when the school was in session. Though in following years the financial conditions were made somewhat less restrictive, up to the outbreak of the 1939–45 war the School Meals Service remained almost exclusively a service for the benefit of necessitous children in Public Elementary schools; and the proportion of children receiving school meals rarely exceeded 3 per cent of the total Elementary School population. Even by 1939 only about half of the LEAs were providing meals.

In 1941 large-scale provision of school meals was decided upon as a means of safeguarding children's health during the war, and great numbers of school canteens were erected. The results of the expanded provision were so obviously beneficial to children that the war-time policy was made permanent national policy. The Education Act 1944 transformed the LEAs' permissive powers into a statutory duty. Section 49 lays down that:

> Regulations made by the Minister shall impose upon local education authorities the duty of providing milk, meals, and other refreshment for pupils in attendance at schools and county colleges maintained by them.

In 1944 it was the Government's declared intention to make school milk, meals and other refreshment a free service; this was to be done, however, not under the Education Acts, but under an Act of Parliament dealing with social security. This Act, the Family Allowances Act, was passed in August 1946; it made the provision of a daily allowance of milk free, but did not legislate for free meals. The argument against doing so was that the School Meals Service had not at the time been extended to a sufficiently large proportion of schools to make it a truly national service. The generally accepted assumption then was that when three-quarters of the schools were receiving the Service the meals would be made free, and their cost would constitute a part of the family allowance granted to parents of children of school age. This assumption has not been realized; in fact, the charge for school meals has risen at intervals ever since. In 1945 the cost to parents was approximately 5d (about 2p) a meal; by 1975 it had risen to 15p.

The price for a school dinner which is charged to the parent is on average rather less than half the total cost of providing the meal. The successive increases in the price of meals had not up to 1976 ever caused more than temporary reductions in the proportion of school-children taking dinners; after rising rapidly during and after the war to over 50 per cent, and then falling slightly, it rose during the ten years 1954–65 from 45.8 per cent to 62.2 per cent. Between 1965 and 1976 it fluctuated between 65 and 70 per cent. Very few maintained Primary and Secondary schools are without facilities for providing cooked meals.

All meals must conform to nutritional standards laid down by the DES. The midday meal ordinarily consists of two courses: a meat dish with (usually) two vegetables followed by a pudding or other sweet. At most schools the meals are cooked on the premises in a specially designed and equipped kitchen staffed by permanent staff. In some places a large school kitchen will cook the meals also for one or more neighbouring schools, and in others the meals for a number of schools will be cooked in a central kitchen; the meals are then put in air-tight containers and distributed by motor vehicle. All new school buildings, and many others, have their own dining hall, though often the whole or part of this has to be used also for other purposes; usually as an assembly hall or a gymnasium. In such conditions the school dinner can be, and often is, a pleasant social gathering. But where the dining space has to be used by classes before and after the meal conditions can be less agreeable.

The part which teachers should play in the supervision of school meals has been since 1944 a matter of recurrent dispute between the teachers' associations and the DES. Section 49 of the Education Act 1944 required the Minister to make Regulations determining "the services to be rendered by managers, governors, and teachers" in the provision of "milk, meals or refreshment". But the Section provided that:

> such regulations shall not impose upon teachers at any school or college . . . duties in respect of meals other than the supervision of pupils.

From the start two issues were involved: whether meal-time supervision made the teacher's day too burdensome, and – much more radical – whether such supervision was part of a teacher's job. In 1945 an attempt was made to resolve the first of these. The Minister issued Regulations laying down that:

> No service by way of supervision shall be required of any teacher and no voluntary assistance to the school meals service shall be given by any teacher, if, in the opinion of the authority, it would adversely affect the quality of the teaching given by that teacher.[2]

The Regulations required each LEA to employ an Organizer of School Meals and "a suitable and adequate staff other than teachers". The primary duties of such staff were the preparation and service of meals, but it was suggested that "to such extent as may be needed" they might assist teachers in the supervision of pupils.[3] In the event, this took little off the teachers' load. In 1957 the NUT took up the matter again, urging the Minister to relieve teachers of all duties in connection with school meals. The Minister replied in 1959 by issuing Circular 349,[4] in which he made various suggestions for easing the teacher's burden. These did not satisfy the teachers' associations, and in 1967 the NUT took direct action, instructing teachers in selected districts to refrain from supervision. As a result, a joint working party representing the DES, the LEAs, and the teachers' associations recommended that supervision be made voluntary. This recommendation the Minister incorporated in Regulations issued in 1968.[5]

It must not be assumed from the foregoing that there has been general dissatisfaction with the School Meals Service itself, which is acknowledged to have proved of immense benefit to children's health, and in many schools a valuable aid to social training. The friction has been over the often unsatisfactory conditions in which meals have had to be taken, and over the part which teachers ought to play in the Service. On the latter question teachers have always been divided; while many believe that teachers ought not to take any part, many others would not willingly sacrifice the opportunities the midday meal offers them for companionship with and training of children. In a very great number of schools the midday meal has always been a happy and useful function.

By Section 78(2) (a) of the Education Act 1944 LEAs may by agreement with the proprietor supply school meals to children in non-maintained – that is, direct grant and independent – schools. The same proviso is made about the cost to the authority of this service as is made about the provision of medical inspection and treatment; that it shall not exceed the *per capita* cost for children in maintained schools.

Milk in Schools Scheme

The provision of milk to children at school, like the provision of meals, was begun by voluntary effort. But its later history was very different. In 1934 the Government granted funds to a Milk Marketing Board (an officially sponsored organization) to launch a 'Milk in Schools Scheme' whereby all children whose parents so desired could have daily one-third of a pint of milk for one halfpenny (less than $\frac{1}{4}$p). Milk for necessitous children (many of whom were given two-thirds of a pint) was paid for by the LEAs. The scheme proved popular, and by 1939 rather more than half of all the children in maintained schools were taking the daily ration. During the 1939–45 war the percentage rose to 70 per cent. In 1946, under the Family Allowances Act, school milk became free to all school-children; as a result the demand for a while rose to over 90 per cent. It later dropped slightly, and in the early 1960s seemed to have become stabilized at about 82 per cent.

In 1968 the Government ended the supply of free milk to Secondary schools, and in 1971 to all pupils over the age of seven, except pupils in Special schools and others for whom doctors recommended it. In late 1976 nearly 94 per cent of pupils entitled by age to free milk were taking it, and 1.6 per cent of older pupils. Over 40 LEAs were selling milk to pupils, mainly of Primary school age.

The normal daily ration is one-third of a pint, except in the case of delicate pupils in Special schools, who may receive two-thirds of a pint. It is given, in maintained schools, on every day on which the school is open for instruction, and is ordinarily taken during the mid-morning break. The milk supplied has to be, so far as possible, pasteurized, or failing that, tuberculin-tested, and the source and supply must be approved by the local authority's Medical Officer of Health. If liquid milk cannot be provided up to the standard required, or cannot be provided at a reasonable cost, the Minister may approve the provision of full-cream dried milk or milk tablets. Pasteurized milk accounts for over 99 per cent of the total supply.

As with school meals, LEAs may make arrangements to supply milk to non-maintained schools.

By Regulations made in 1959[6] the cost of the School Milk and Meals Services was excluded from the block grant made by the Government to LEAs. Until 31 March 1967 the DES continued to pay 100 per cent grant in respect of the expenditure incurred by a local authority in providing these two services. Under the Local Government Act 1966 school meals and milk ceased from 1 April 1967 to rank for 100 per cent grant from the Exchequer. Instead, LEAs received grants for these Services, as for all their expenditure, through the Rate Support Grant (RSG) introduced by this Act.

Boarding Accommodation

Section 8(2)(d) of the Education Act 1944 requires LEAs to have particular regard to:

the expediency of securing the provision of boarding accommodation, either in boarding-schools or otherwise, for pupils for whom education as boarders is considered by their parents and by the authority to be desirable.

The power to provide boarding-schools was a new one. Several LEAs – notably London and Surrey – established boarding Secondary schools, and others attached boarding-houses or hostels to schools mainly for day pupils. Boarding-houses and hostels are principally intended to spare children long daily journeys. Boarding-schools give priority to children whose parents are working overseas or whose employment keeps them moving from place to place, and to children who (usually because of unsatisfactory home circumstances) cannot be altogether satisfactorily educated in a day-school.

Section 50(1) of the Education Act 1944 empowers LEAs to provide boarding accommodation, not in a school or county college, in order to enable a pupil to attend a particular school or college judged by the authority to be specially suitable for him. This power is extensively used for pupils requiring special educational treatment. Sub-section (2) of this Section requires the authority, "so far as practicable", to give effect to parents' wishes about the denominational character of the school.

Clothing of Pupils

Section 51 of the Education Act 1944 gives LEAs power to provide a child with clothing if in their opinion he "is unable by reason of the inadequacy of his clothing to take full advantage of the education provided at the school". This power also was granted for the first time in 1944. It has not had to be widely used. Section 52 empowers LEAs to recover from parents all or part of the cost of the clothing. Section 53(3) allows the Minister to make Regulations, which he early did,[7] empowering LEAs to provide for pupils at maintained schools or county colleges "such articles of clothing suitable for the physical training provided . . . as may be prescribed". This power has been fairly widely used in schools.

Cleanliness of Pupils

Section 54 of the Education Act 1944 empowers LEAs to have pupils' persons and clothing examined in the interests of cleanliness by a medical officer, to exclude from school any pupil whose body or clothing is so foul that it constitutes a nuisance, or who is infested with vermin, to require the parent to have the child properly cleansed or, failing that, to undertake the cleansing themselves. This is a power that has not had to be extensively used, though infestation, especially of the hair, remains persistent in some districts, especially where housing is old and sub-standard. But many schools have not had a verminous child for years.

Careers Service

Between 1948 and 1974 vocational guidance for children and young people was the function of a Youth Employment Service responsible to the Ministry of Labour (later the Department of Employment and Productivity) but operated locally, in most areas, by LEAs. The Service, which was available throughout Great Britain, was administered centrally by a Central Youth Employment Executive, and the Minister was advised by a National Youth Employment Council for England and by Advisory Committees for Scotland and Wales. The Service had three functions: vocational guidance, assistance in finding employment, and after-care of young employees up to the age of 18. In support of the first of these the Central Executive maintained a careers research section which published a comprehensive series of 'Choice of Careers' booklets.

The Employment and Training Act 1973, which came into operation on 1 April 1974, ended this system, and made it the duty of all LEAs to provide a Careers Service for all persons, of any age, who are attending an educational institution. The LEAs were given freedom to decide what kind of organization they would have. Financial aid from the Treasury comes through the Rate Support Grant, the previous specific grant of 75 per cent being abolished.

References

1 *The Health of the School Child*: Report of the Chief Medical Officer of the Ministry of Education for the years 1956 and 1957. Chapter VIII.
2 *The Milk and Meals Regulations 1945* (SR and O 1945, No. 698), Regulation 14(c).
3 ibid, Regulation 13.
4 *The School Meals Service and the Teacher*, dated 20 March 1959.
5 *The Provision of Milk and Meals (Amendment No. 2) Regulations 1968* (SI 1968, No. 1251), dated 16 August 1968.
6 *The Milk and Meals Grant Regulations 1959* (SI 1959, No. 410), which came into operation on 1 April 1959.
7 *The Physical Training (Clothing) Regulations 1945* (SR and O 1945, No. 371).

Further reading

School Health Services

MONCRIEFF, A., *Child Health and the State*. Oxford University Press, 1953.

Official
Ministry of Education. *Education 1900–1950*: Report of the Ministry of Education for the year 1950. (Chapter 6): and other annual reports, and, from 1968, the annual report of the Chief Medical Officer of the Department of Health and Social Security.
The Health of the School Child. Published biennially.
Handbook of Health Education, 1968.
Psychologists in Education Services ('Summerfield' Report), 1968.
HENDERSON, PETER, *The School Health Service 1908–1974*. DES, 1975.
   All from H.M. Stationery Office.

School Meals

CLARK, F. LE G., *Social History of the School Meals Service*. National Council of Social Service, 1948. (Pamphlet.)
Ministry of Education. *Report of an Inquiry into the Working of the School Meals Service* (1955–1956), 1956. (Pamphlet.)
Ministry of Social Security. *Circumstances of Families*, 1967.
N.U.T. *Survey of the School Meals Service*. 1956.
Catering in Schools: Report of the Committee on Catering Arrangements in Schools. HMSO, 1975.

Nutrition in Schools: Report of the Working Party on the Nutritional Aspects of School Meals. HMSO, 1975.

Youth Employment Service

CARTER, M. P., *Home, School and Work*: A Study of the Education and Employment of Young People in Britain. Pergamon Press, 1962.

Official

The Future Development of the Youth Employment Service. Report of a Working Party of the National Youth Employment Council (The 'Albemarle' Report). H.M. Stationery Office, 1965.

Ministry of Labour and National Service. *Youth Employment Service* (Memorandum on exercise of powers by LEAs).

Careers Guidance and Employment: Careers Education in the 1970s. Schools Council Working Paper No. 40, Evans/Methuen, 1972.

CHAPTER 8 | # Independent Schools

The title 'Independent school' is preferred here to 'Private school', for two reasons: first, because it is the term used in the Education Act 1944, and secondly, because many of the schools in this category are not 'private' in the sense of being the absolute property of private owners; they are conducted under the terms of trusts and administered by duly constituted boards of trustees or governors.

Even the term 'Independent' is not today wholly accurate. The schools here to be described are 'independent' in that they have to be financially self-supporting; no school in this extremely heterogeneous group receives any direct subvention from public funds. But none is exempt from State control. Part III (Sections 70–75) of the Education Act 1944, which came into operation on 30 September 1957, requires that every independent school shall be registered with the DES, and gives the Secretary of State the power (subject to appeal) to close any school he deems to be in unsuitable premises, to be providing inadequate or unsuitable accommodation, to be giving inefficient or unsuitable instruction, or to be conducted by persons not fit to be in charge of or teaching in a school. It is a legal offence to open or conduct an unregistered school.

Section 114 of the Education Act 1944 defines an "Independent school" as:

any school at which full-time education is provided for five or more pupils of compulsory school age (whether or not such education is also provided for pupils under or over that age), not being a school maintained by a local education authority or a school in respect of which grants are made by the Minister to the proprietor of the school.

The word 'proprietor' is defined (in the same section of the Act) as "the person or body of persons responsible for the management of the school".

The independent schools in England and Wales may be classified in various ways. A distinction is frequently drawn between the so-called 'Public' schools and those which are not accorded this title. Not without reason, but it is essential to point out that not all 'Public' schools are independent schools. The conditions governing the grant of the title will be outlined later; suffice to say here that a school's financial basis is not one of them.

The origin of the term 'Public School' is disputed. It may go back to the fourteenth century, but a simple derivation of present-day usage is found in the fact that towards the end of the eighteenth century a few boarding-schools for boys gradually became known as the 'Great' or 'Public' schools, and that they were given the latter title because they were open to boys from all over the country (and beyond it), and not restricted to boys living in the immediate locality. These schools were few in number; as late as 1864 a Royal Commission (the 'Clarendon' Commission) recognized only nine: Eton, Winchester, Westminster, Charterhouse, Harrow, Rugby, Shrewsbury, St. Paul's, and Merchant Taylors. In the legislation which followed in 1868 the last two of these schools, which were day-schools, were omitted, and so for a while only the other seven schools were officially recognized as 'Public' schools.

Between 1864 and 1868 another Royal Commission (the 'Schools Inquiry' or 'Taunton' Commission) investigated the affairs of all the endowed schools not investigated by the 'Clarendon' Commission. In 1869 Parliament incorporated some of its recommendations in an Endowed Schools Act. This established an Endowed Schools Commission, which was empowered to modify the constitutions of schools, to make new schemes where necessary, and to divert to appropriate educational purposes trust funds whose original purposes had become obsolete.

Many heads of endowed schools feared that the independence of their schools could be endangered by the Commission. A group of about twenty-five of them met to discuss the situation, and as a result the Rev Edward Thring, headmaster of Uppingham School, wrote to the heads of thirty-seven of the leading boys' Grammar schools, suggesting that they should establish an annual conference to defend their freedom. The response to his letter was disappointing; only twelve headmasters (and none from the seven 'Public' schools) attended the first conference. By the following year, however, there was a change of heart; thirty-four headmasters turned up, including the heads of all the 'Public' schools. At this meeting a committee was elected consisting of the headmasters of Eton, Winchester, Harrow, Repton, Cheltenham, Clifton, Uppingham, the City of London School, and Sherborne. And so, as Mr Vivian Ogilvie says in his attractive book *The English Public School*:

> Every genus of the species Public school was thus represented – the old aristocrats, the glorified grammar schools of both vintages, the large city day schools and the new foundations.

The 'Headmasters' Conference' thus established, Mr Ogilvie goes on to say:

> . . . registered the fact, albeit unintentionally, that a certain number of schools, varying in origin and character, enjoyed a degree of prosperity and esteem that marked them off from the majority of the old endowed Grammar schools.[1]

That was how the term 'Public school' became extended to cover more schools than the original nine. Since that meeting any school has been entitled to describe itself as a 'Public school' if its headmaster is elected a member of the Headmasters' Conference (HMC). Until 1941 this was the only means of gaining the title. In that year the Association of Governing Bodies of Public Schools (GBA) was formed, and in the following year the President of the Board of Education, Mr R. A. Butler, acknowledged that membership of the GBA conferred the title of 'Public school'; in appointing a committee (the 'Fleming' Committee) to consider the relationship of the Public schools to the general educational system of the country he defined Public schools as "schools which are in membership of the Governing Bodies' Association or Headmasters' Conference".

That was the only official definition of a Public school up to 1965. Then, the Government appointed a Public Schools Commission, under the chairmanship of Sir John Newsom, "to advise on the best way of integrating the public schools with the state system". In the Commission's terms of reference public schools were defined as:

> those independent schools now in membership of the Headmasters' Conference, Governing Bodies Association or Governing Bodies of Girls Schools Associations.

These definitions carry no statutory sanction. The title 'Public school' is a courtesy title only, though one so firmly established and respected that no school not in membership of one of the above associations would dream of assuming it.

The first report of the Public Schools Commission was published in July 1968. It declared independent schools to be a divisive influence in society, and recommended a scheme of integration whereby "suitable boarding-schools (with which the Commission had been particularly concerned) would make over at least half of their places to assisted pupils who need boarding education". Public reactions were mainly hostile. In March 1970 a reconstituted commission, under the chairmanship of Professor D. V. Donnison (previously vice-chairman), presented a second report, on direct grant Grammar schools and independent day schools. It recommended that all such schools wishing to work within the national system of education should go comprehensive and abolish tuition fees.

However much the title 'Public school' may be a courtesy title it is nevertheless an extremely difficult one to secure, and some of the conditions of obtaining it are quite rigid. It has never been granted to any but Secondary schools. HMC will admit boys' schools only, and limits its membership to about 200, apart from Associates and Overseas members. Both HMC and GBA have so far admitted only Grammar schools. The constitution of HMC "provides that the membership shall consist mainly of headmasters of Independent and Direct Grant Schools". A "small number" of heads of Voluntary and Maintained schools may also be elected. In considering applications for election the Committee has regard to "the degree of independence enjoyed by the Headmaster and his school . . . [and] the academic standards obtaining in the school, as reflected by the proportion of boys in the Sixth form pursuing a course of study beyond the Ordinary level of the General Certificate of Education.[2]

The GBA will admit to membership "Governing Bodies of Schools for Boys (including co-educational schools) in the British Isles (a) receiving no grants from public monies (called 'Independent Schools'), (b) receiving direct grant from the Department of Education and Science or equivalent authority in Scotland or Northern Ireland (called 'Direct Grant Schools')".[3] It may also admit on its own conditions, schools not so qualified.

It will be seen that by definition neither the HMC or the GBA restricts itself to Independent schools. Actually, up to 1976, when the category of direct-grant Grammar schools ceased to exist, about one-third of the membership of each body consisted of grant-aided schools. Most were Direct-Grant schools, but the lists included also Voluntary Aided and Controlled schools in England and Wales. The HMC and GBA lists, in fact, largely comprised the same schools. Girls' schools have always been much less exclusively segregated and it is only of recent years that the title 'Public School' has become at all common among them.

Within the heterogeneous group of boys' 'Public' schools there has always been, and still is, an inner circle of more famous, more highly reputed and – though to a lesser degree today than ever before – more exclusive schools. What the Clarendon Commission said of 'the Nine' over a century ago remains substantially true today:

> From the prominent positions they have long occupied as places of instruction for the wealthier classes, and from the general but by no means exact resemblance of their system of discipline and teaching, they have become especially identified with what in this country is commonly called Public School Education . . . [which], as it exists in England and in England alone, has grown up chiefly within their walls and has been propagated from them; and, though now surrounded by younger institutions of a like character, and of great and increasing importance, they are still, in common estimation, its acknowledged types, as they have for several generations been its principal centres.[4]

Opinions would differ about precisely how many (and which) schools should today be included in this inner circle; but it is safe to say that their number would not greatly exceed the nine of the Clarendon Commission. It is, in fact, possible to distinguish at least four groups of schools among those on the HMC list: the inner circle; a second group, principally of boarding-schools, which has achieved a national reputation; a third, again principally of boarding-schools, which has attained the title largely by studiously imitating the 'acknowledged types'; and a fourth which, starting from humble origins, has earned the title by sheer educational merit. Included in this last group are many day-schools.

Of the schools on the HMC list in 1976 over 100 are predominantly boarding-schools, though many of these admit also day boys. Over 50 are predominantly day-schools, though again some of these include boarders. Among both boarding- and day-schools the proportion of ancient foundations is very large; and interestingly enough is larger among the day- than the boarding-schools.

Sixty per cent of the boarding-schools were founded before the nineteenth century, and eighty per cent of the day schools.

About a dozen of the independent boarding-schools are on religious foundations. The Roman Catholic schools at Ampleforth near York, Douai near Reading, and Downside near Bath, were all founded, and are conducted, by the Benedictine order. Among Anglican schools are those founded by the Rev Nathaniel Woodard (examples are Lancing and Worksop) "to provide at moderate cost a public school education on the principles of the Church of England". Kingswood, at Bath, was founded by the Rev John Wesley for the sons of his itinerant preachers; it still has close ties with the Methodist Church. Leighton Park at Reading was founded by, and is under the direction of, the Society of Friends.

Most of the 'Public' schools owe their origin to endowments made by private individuals or corporate bodies. This is not entirely true of a few of the oldest schools, which were founded by the Church, and for centuries remained part of it; but even these schools were re-founded, or revived, at much later dates. The King's School, at Canterbury, for example, which is practically certainly the lineal descendant of a school founded by St Augustine about A.D. 597, was re-established and re-endowed by King Henry VIII in 1541. Similarly, St Peter's, York, the successor to a Royal School of St Peter which came into being in the seventh century, was re-founded and re-endowed by Queen Mary Tudor and her husband King Philip of Spain. Many of the older schools were founded jointly with other charities; examples are Charterhouse, founded by Thomas Sutton in 1609 along with almshouses for old men (which still exist), and Christ's Hospital, founded by King Edward VI in 1552. A number were founded, and are still managed, by craft or merchant guilds; among these the Merchant Taylors' schools at Northwood in Middlesex and Crosby in Lancashire still bear the name of their founding body. The Haberdashers' Aske's School in London is unique in bearing the names both of its individual founder, Robert Aske, and of the guild to which he belonged and to which he bequeathed the funds for the founding of the school.

As has been recorded in Chapter 1, the oldest known example of a school founded specifically as a school is Winchester College. The example was frequently copied; but few of the medieval foundations made, as did Winchester and Eton, provision in their foundation deeds for boarders. More old schools than is generally realized have remained day-schools. Well-known examples are St Paul's School in London, founded by John Colet, Dean of St Paul's Cathedral, in 1509 (this foundation probably absorbed an older cathedral school), and Manchester Grammar School, founded six years later by Hugh Oldham, Bishop of Exeter. But there are throughout the country hundreds of other such schools: to give but one example, Stockport Grammar school, founded in 1487 by Sir Edmund Shaa, Lord Mayor of London and a prominent member of the Goldsmiths' Company. The foundation of schools slackened in the latter part of the seventeenth century, and was particularly infrequent during the eighteenth. The rapid development of England as an industrial country during the first half of the nineteenth century led to a fresh outburst which reached its climax between about 1840 and 1860. Examples of schools founded then for the education of middle-class boys are Cheltenham College (1841), Clifton College (1862), Malvern College (1862), and Marlborough (1843). Some of these schools (like those on the Woodard foundation) were founded with a specific religious purpose; among them is Brighton College (1845), founded by residents of the town to provide "a thoroughly liberal and practical education in conformity with the principles of the Established Church". An interesting example of a quite different specific purpose is Llandovery College, founded and endowed in 1848 by Sir Thomas Phillips to be a Church school in which Welsh boys could "study their own language, history and literature, as part of a sound classical and liberal education".

Only a very few Public schools are twentieth century foundations. Stowe, in Buckinghamshire (1923), is one, and Bryanston, at Blandford in Dorset (1928), another. Both these were designed to be Public schools, but to incorporate new features. Bryanston's aim was to combine "what is best in the Old Public School tradition with what experiment has shown to be sound in more modern educational systems". Milton Abbey (1954) emphasizes personal qualities in selecting entrants.

The 'Old Public School tradition', which has made a group of English schools famous throughout the world, is largely a nineteenth century creation. Its birth is usually attributed to Thomas Arnold, headmaster of Rugby School from 1828 to 1842, but modern research has shown that, while he must still be regarded as the greatest among the reforming headmasters who transformed the English Public schools from being "the seed beds of. . . the less attractive characteristics of mankind", into places devoted to the building of sound character through "responsible living, based on the ethos of the total community and reinforced and directed by the headmaster's authority and guidance",[5] there were predecessors who paved the way for him, and successors who, by enlarging and extending his concepts, built the tradition into a system.

Direct Grant Schools

In 1926 schools which were grant-aided, but not maintained by LEAs, and some independent schools which were governed by schemes made under the Endowed Schools Acts, were given the option of receiving grant direct from the Board of Education, subject to specified conditions about the acceptance of pupils and the tuition fees charged. This arrangement, which left the schools a considerable amount of independence, persisted for fifty years, despite recurrent criticism of it.

There were in 1975 about 300 'Direct Grant' schools. Of these, 174 were Grammar schools; most of the others were Special schools. The conditions on which they received grant were laid down in Regulations made by the Secretary of State.[6] In brief, the Grammar schools – the object of the criticism – had to offer at least one-quarter of their annual entry (except of pupils under the age of ten) to pupils from maintained Primary schools, whose tuition fees would be paid by either the governors of the school or the LEA. If LEAs wanted more places the governors had to make available to them up to another 25 per cent; these were called 'reserved' places. For other pupils the governors could charge tuition fees; but the amount had to be approved by the Secretary of State, who had also the right to remit or reduce the amount of the fees paid by individual parents. In return for meeting these and other conditions, Direct Grant schools received a capitation grant in respect of each pupil aged ten or over, together with an additional grant in respect of each pupil in the sixth form. The amount of the grants, and the parental income scales on which remissions of fees were based, were periodically adjusted.

When the Education Act 1944 abolished fee-paying in maintained schools, many people felt that it should be abolished also in direct-grant schools. An attempt to effect this was made while the Bill was passing through Parliament, but it was unsuccessful, and nothing was done until May 1975, when the Labour Government asked the 174 Direct Grant Grammar schools to decide, by the end of the year, whether they wished to join the maintained sector, and so become Comprehensive, or not. By December over 100 schools had decided to become independent, and 51 (mainly Roman Catholic schools) to become maintained. Those which opted for independence ceased to receive grant from August 1976. The rights of the pupils already in the schools were safeguarded.[7]

Preparatory Schools

'Preparatory', or 'Prep' schools, as they are familiarly called, prepare boys[8] for entry into independent Public schools. Many are privately owned, but in recent years a great number have transferred the ownership to a board of trustees. Many are wholly or partly boarding schools, but in 1976 about two-thirds of Prep school pupils were day pupils. Prep schools accept pupils from about the age of eight or nine and keep them until about thirteen and a half. About 450 of these schools, containing in 1976 about 72,000 pupils, are linked together by membership of the Incorporated Association of Preparatory Schools (IAPS), founded in 1892. This Association keeps an eye on academic and other standards in the schools (all IAPS schools must be 'Recognized as Efficient' by the DES), arranges transfers, amalgamations and partnerships, runs an appointments bureau and a pension scheme for assistant teachers, provides legal assistance for its members, and organizes training courses for teachers in Preparatory schools. It keeps in close touch with the Public schools' associations through the Independent Schools' Joint Committee, established in 1974 to consider matters of policy and administration common to its memberships. Among these matters is the Common Entrance Examination for entry into an independent Public school (entry into a maintained school is subject to regulations made by the Secretary of State). The Common Entrance Examination is taken by boys between the ages of twelve and fourteen and must be passed in order to secure entry to an independent Public school. There are two levels of pass: for securing entry, and for securing one of the many open scholarships awarded by Public schools.

The following scheme of examination was in operation in 1976.[9]

GROUP A– *Compulsory papers*
English I and II.
Mathematics I and II.
French (written).

GROUP B – *Compulsory supporting papers*
History, Geography.
Scripture, Science.

GROUP C – *Optional papers*
Latin, Greek.
Mathematics III, French (oral).

The age of transfer from Preparatory school to independent Public school, and the existence of Latin and Greek in the Preparatory school curriculum, are among the stubborn facts which make integration of the independent and maintained systems formidably difficult.

Other Independent Schools

Since compulsory registration of independent schools came into operation in 1957 the number of independent schools, and of pupils in such schools, has greatly decreased. In 1959 there were about 4,250 schools containing about 500,000 pupils; by 1975 the number of schools had been halved, and the number of pupils had fallen by one-fifth. The loss had been almost entirely among the smaller and weaker schools. The number of independent 'Public' schools was unchanged, and the number of their pupils had increased. The number of schools which, by voluntarily undergoing more rigorous inspection than is required for registration, had earned from DES the appellation 'Recognized as Efficient', had also increased. But the number of unrecognized schools had decreased substantially. Many of these were very small schools (under 50 pupils), and many were schools for children of primary school age only.

It must be made clear that not being 'Recognized as Efficient' does not imply that a school is inefficient. There are many well-known schools of good reputation which for one reason or another do not seek recognition, preferring the rather larger freedom which non-recognition allows.

The non-Public independent schools have their own professional associations. Among these is the Independent Schools Association Inc., membership of which is open to the Head of any school not receiving grant from the State. It has about 500 members.

References

1 Ogilvie, Vivian, *The English Public School*. Batsford, 1957, p. 167.
2 *The Public and Preparatory Schools Year Book*. A. & C. Black, 1976 edition, p. xx.
3 ibid, p. xxiii.
4 Quoted from Ogilvie, op. cit. pp. 5–6.
5 Professor E. B. Castle, in *The Year Book of Education 1958*. Evans Bros, pp. 7 and 8.
6 *The Direct Grant Schools Regulations 1959* (SI 1959, No. 1832).
7 *The Direct Grant Grammar Schools (Cessation of Grant) Regulations 1975*.
8 In recent years some have begun to accept girls also.
9 Some heads were in 1976 pressing for revision of the examination.

Further Reading

A. & C. BLACK (publishers), *The Public and Preparatory Schools' Year Book*.
The Independent Schools Association Year Book.
The Girls' School Year Book.
BOYD, W., and RAWSON, W., *The Story of the New Education*. Heinemann, 1965.
KALTON, GRAHAM, *The Public Schools*. A Factual Survey. Longmans, 1966.
MASTERS, PHILIP L., *Preparatory Schools Today*. Some Facts and Inferences. A. & C. Black, 1966.
OGILVIE, VIVIAN, *The English Public School*. Batsford, 1957.
STEWART, W. A. C., and MCCANN, W. P., *The Educational Innovators*. Volume I: 1750–1880. Macmillan, 1967. Volume II: Progressive Schools 1881–1967 (by W. A. C. STEWART). Macmillan, 1968.

Official

Ministry of Education. *The Public Schools and the General Educational System* ('Fleming' Report), 1944.
Annual Report for 1958 (*Education in 1958*) which contains a survey of Independent schools in that year.
(Both from HM Stationery Office.)
Department of Education and Science. *The Public Schools Commission: First Report*. Volume 1. Report, Volume 2. Appendix. 1968. *Second Report*. Volume 1, Report on Independent Days Schools and Direct Grant Schools. 1970. HM Stationery Office.

CHAPTER 9 | Further Education

The term 'Further Education' was introduced into legislation by the Education Act 1944, with a different meaning from that of any term previously used. (The 'Higher Education' which the pre-1944 LEAs were empowered to provide was any form of education, other than university education, beyond elementary education.)

> Further Education is defined by Section 41 of the 1944 Act as:
> (a) full-time and part-time education for persons over compulsory school age; and
> (b) leisure-time occupation, in such organized cultural training and recreative activities as are suited to their requirements, for any persons over compulsory school age who are able and willing to profit by the facilities provided for the purpose.

It will be seen that the potential range and variety of Further Education (FE) can be very great; and, in fact, both are. In the field of formal education every level of attainment is provided for from that of the boy or girl of modest ability who has just left a Secondary school at the age of sixteen to that of the post-graduate student; and practically every field of knowledge or skill which is the subject of serious study is covered. Similarly, in the field of informal education virtually every worth-while leisure-time activity finds a place.

Since the publication in 1963 of the 'Robbins' Report on *Higher Education* there has been a growing tendency to distinguish between 'Further' and 'Higher' education. The latter comprises (in the words of the Report) "courses for the education and training of teachers or systematic courses of further education beyond the Advanced level of the General Certificate of Education or beyond the Ordinary National Certificate or its equivalent".[1] Subsequent developments made this distinction important; but it has no statutory sanction.

Before the varied provision of Further Education is described, three general points should be made. First, FE is not compulsory. Except for a brief period between 1920 and 1922, and for much longer at a single college,[2] no one in England and Wales has been under any statutory obligation to take part in any educational activity after leaving school. In this respect practice lags behind legislation. The Education Act 1918 provided for a scheme of compulsory part-time education in 'Day Continuation Schools' for all young people beyond compulsory school age who had not attained the age of eighteen and were not undertaking other recognized forms of full- or part-time education. This provision was re-affirmed in the Education Act 1921, and nearly a quarter of a century later in the Education Act 1944 (in which the Day Continuation Schools were called 'County Colleges'), but thirty-three years after that last Act it is still not implemented – and seems unlikely to be in the foreseeable future.

Secondly, although FE is entirely a voluntary activity, all LEAs are under a statutory obligation to ensure that adequate and efficient facilities for it are available in their areas. Thirdly, whatever defects there may be in provision (and no one would deny that there are many), FE in England and Wales has one pervading virtue; it is so flexibly organized that a student may enter it at any level, and progress within it so far as his capacity will carry him.

Most FE is provided by the LEAs, and the total bulk of their provision is impressively large. In 1975–6 they were maintaining or grant-aiding 30 Polytechnics, nearly 600 other major colleges, nearly 7,000 Evening Institutes and 30 residential Colleges and Centres of Adult Education. The major establishments were attended by nearly two million students, of whom about 390,000 were following full-time courses (continuous or 'sandwich'), and about 740,000 part-time day courses. Over two and three-quarter million students were attending evening classes. The short courses at the Colleges and Centres of Adult Education attracted over 80,000 students. Thus crudely stated, these figures may be misleading. Though the evening students were far more numerous than the full- and part-time day students, the number of hours they put in was considerably less; and this is indicative of one of the most significant changes in the structure of FE that has taken place since the Second World War: the transfer of studies related to vocation from the evening to the working day.

The provision made by the LEAs is supplemented by that of (*a*) a few (but important) colleges in receipt of direct grant from the DES, (*b*) voluntary bodies, and (*c*) commercial, industrial, and professional associations and establishments. Four outstanding direct grant colleges[3] provide highly specialized vocational education. The provision made by voluntary bodies falls largely into two fields: non-vocational 'Adult Education', and social and recreational facilities for young people. That made by private enterprise is concerned almost entirely with vocational education, and comprises: (1) from professional associations, co-operation in examining, and (2) from industrial and commercial establishments the maintenance of education and training departments for their employees (and sometimes those of other firms as well). There are also about 100 independent colleges which are recognized as efficient by the DES. A great number of their students are foreigners learning English as a second language.

Section 41 of the Education Act 1944 draws a clear distinction between FE conducted formally in classes organized for instructional purposes – that is what "full-time and part-time education" means – and informal FE, that is "leisure-time occupation" in "organized cultural training and recreative activities". But in order really to understand the structure of FE in England and Wales one should think of it as divided into three broad fields: vocational education, that is, education directly related to specific employments; formal 'Adult Education'; and social and recreative activities. These fields overlap here and there; it would be possible, for example, to find in a modern languages class students who are there for strictly vocational purposes, students who are learning a foreign language as a liberal study, and students who are there because to learn a language other than their own is an enjoyable 'leisure-time occupation'. Similarly, in an elementary cookery class may be found students hoping ultimately to become chefs, housewives wanting to improve the quality of the family's meals, and students who find cooking a delightful hobby. Such examples could be multiplied. Nevertheless, the three fields are in general sharply distinguished from each other.

By far the greatest numbers of students in LEA Colleges of Further Education are taking vocational courses. Among full-time and part-time day students most are doing so. Many follow courses leading to named qualifications: CNAA degrees, National Certificates and Diplomas, awards made by professional associations, Certificates of the City and Guilds of London Institute, and – not least – the General Certificate of Education (GCE).

The generic term 'vocational education' is not greatly used in England; we prefer the more particular terms 'technical', 'technological', 'commercial', 'art', 'agricultural', and 'professional' education. Though these terms appear to be more precise, the first has tended – and still tends – to obscure rather than clarify. Many FE Colleges are still called Technical Colleges, though most of them include in their programme subjects which cannot strictly be called 'technical'. Moreover, in the words of a former college principal, "the term technical education has no precise meaning either administratively or educationally".[4] With the increasing use of the terms 'technology', 'technologist' and 'technological education', however, it is tending more and more to mean vocational education for industrial workers which does not lead to qualifications giving professional status. The term 'technological education' is generally used to mean courses of vocational education leading directly to professional status in an industrial occupation.

Since the passing of the Education Act 1944 a series of radical changes has been made in the structure of FE and the functions of FE colleges. In the 1950s the provision of technical and technological education in England and Wales was rationalized to form a pyramidal edifice of four storeys. As it had grown up more or less haphazardly, most FE colleges were offering courses at many levels; but following the publication in 1956 of a White Paper, entitled *Technical Education*, the process of segregating the more advanced from the more elementary work, which had been proceeding slowly and unevenly for years, was greatly expedited, and carried out systematically all over the country.

At the apex of the four-tier pyramid were ten Colleges of Advanced Technology (CATs),[5] which have since been made universities, or, in two cases, colleges of existing universities.[6] The CATs were devoted entirely to advanced studies, including courses leading to a Diploma in Technology (Dip Tech)

GCE O-level engineering drawing in a college of further education

which was created in 1956 to be for students in non-university colleges the equivalent of a university first degree with honours. Up to 1965, when the Dip Tech was superseded by the degrees of the Council for National Academic Awards (CNAA), the Diploma attracted rapidly increasing numbers of students – in 1964 nearly 9,000. A higher award, Membership of the College of Technologists (MCT), was established in 1959. Intended to be comparable with a PhD, it was awarded for programmes of original work carried out jointly in a non-university college and industry on problems of potential industrial interest. Like the Dip Tech, it was superseded by the CNAA degrees.

The second tier in the technical pyramid was tenanted by some twenty-five Regional Colleges. They, like the CATs, were occupied largely with advanced courses. They also offered courses in scientific and technological subjects for which the numerical demand was relatively slight, and for which students had to be drawn from a wide area. For this reason, and because of their many full-time students, some of the Regional Colleges had Halls of Residence. As in the CATs, many of their full-time students attended on a 'sandwich' basis, that is, they spent alternate periods of some months' duration in college and in employment.[7] Such students may be 'college-based' or 'industry-based'. In the first case they register with a college, which places them with a firm, or firms; in the second they become employees of a firm, which places them with a college.

The third tier was occupied by the Area Colleges. These, the main local colleges in the areas of LEAs, handle work at an intermediate level, leaving more elementary studies to District Colleges. A principal task of Area Colleges is the preparation of students, and in particular part-time day students released by their employers, for the examinations leading to Ordinary National Certificates and to the certificates awarded by the City and Guilds of London Institute.

In 1963 the 'Robbins' Report on *Higher Education*[8] recommended that the CATs should become universities, and this recommendation was implemented in 1966–67. In 1965 the Secretary of State for Education and Science, Mr Anthony Crosland, advocated in a speech at Woolwich a 'binary' system of Higher Education comprising an 'autonomous' sector (i.e. the universities), financed by the UGC, and a 'public' sector consisting of colleges financed by the LEAs. In 1966 the Government announced, in a White Paper entitled *A Plan for Polytechnics and Other Colleges*,[9] that it intended to provide a new top level institution for the public sector by creating a limited number (which later proved to be 30) of 'Polytechnics', mainly by amalgamations of existing colleges. These Polytechnics were to be comprehensive academic communities catering for full-time, sandwich, and part-time students, and providing for them all sorts of courses at all levels of Higher Education. By 1973 all the 30 Polytechnics had been established and were at work.

In 1972 the 'James' Report on *Teacher Education and Training*[10] proposed a radically new scheme for the training of teachers, arranged in three 'cycles' of general education, pre-service professional training, and in-service education and training. The reaction to this Report was mixed, and to some parts of it hostile, so not surprisingly the Government did not accept the whole of its proposed scheme. Elements of it were, however, incorporated in a White Paper, *Education: A Framework for Expansion*,[11] which the Government issued in December 1972. This, as its title suggests, covered the whole range of public education, and included university education. Its most radical proposals concerned the training of teachers which it said should be fully incorporated into the public sector of Higher Education. Colleges of Education would cease to be devoted solely to the training of teachers; they would accept students not committed to teaching, and provide for them courses which could lead to other careers. Because the birthrate had been falling since 1964, the number of teachers to be trained would be progressively reduced to bring the annual intake down to about half the 1972 figure. This meant that some Colleges of Education would have to be closed, or diverted to other purposes. The process of reorganization outlined in the White Paper began in 1974, but was still far from complete by the end of 1976.[12]

Non-University Degrees

In September 1964 a revolutionary innovation was made: by Royal Charter there was established a Council for National Academic Awards (CNAA), which was to be:

. . . an autonomous body with powers to award first and higher degrees, diplomas, and other academic distinctions to persons who have successfully pursued courses or undertaken research work approved by the Council at an educational or research establishment other than a university.[13]

Thus for the first time in the history of Great Britain (the Council's writ extends to Scotland) the power to confer degrees of all kinds was entrusted to a body other than a university.[14] It is required that CNAA degrees shall be comparable in standard with those conferred by universities. Academic qualifications for entry into CNAA first degree courses are, in terms of the GCE or the Scottish Certificate of Education, similar to those required by Universities; but the Council accepts also a good Ordinary National Certificate or Ordinary National Diploma. The degrees being awarded by the CNAA in 1976 were: Bachelor of Arts (BA), Bachelor of Science (BSc), Master of Arts (MA), Master of Science (MSc), Master of Philosophy (MPhil), Doctor of Philosophy (PhD).

National Certificates and Diplomas

National Certificates and Diplomas are technicians' qualifications. They are offered in many scientific and technological subjects, and in business studies. The Certificates can be obtained only by part-time study, the Diplomas only by full-time (including 'sandwich'). Both are awarded at two levels, Ordinary and Higher. The standard of an Ordinary National Certificate (ONC) or an Ordinary National Diploma (OND) is regarded as comparable with that of GCE 'A' level. A Higher National Diploma (HND) is rated as equivalent to a pass degree, a Higher National Certificate (HNC) as somewhat lower. Both Certificates and Diplomas are awarded jointly by the DES and the professional association concerned. They approve syllabuses drawn up by individual colleges, and appoint moderators for examinations set and marked by the colleges.

This system began in 1920–21. During the years between the first and second world wars it grew steadily, if slowly. Certificate students were always much more numerous than Diploma. By 1938 they were obtaining annually about 3,300 Ordinary and 1,100 Higher Certificates. After 1944 the range of subjects was progressively widened, and the numbers of Certificates and Diplomas obtained increased spectacularly. By the mid-1970s over 80,000 students would be on Certificate courses, and about half as many on Diploma. But in both cases, and more particularly among Certificate students, the dropout rate was alarmingly high. In 1962, in accordance with recommendations made in a White Paper, *Better Opportunities in Technical Education*, issued in 1961,[15] preparatory general courses were introduced for school-leavers who did not possess the academic qualifications required for entry into an ONC or OND course. That did not, unfortunately, solve the problem. In 1969 a Committee on Technician Courses and Examinations, set up by the NACEIC at the request of the

Part-time day release students on a catering course

Secretary of State (the 'Haslegrave' Committee),[16] recommended that he should establish a Technician Education Council (TEC) and a Business Education Council (BEC), "to plan, co-ordinate and administer national technician and comparable examinations and qualifications". The committee also proposed that a unified pattern of courses should be gradually introduced which would ultimately replace the National Certificate/Diploma pattern, along with that of the City and Guilds of London Institute (CGLI). There was some delay in implementing these recommendations; the TEC was set up in 1973 and the BEC in 1974. In 1974 the TEC announced that it would make two awards, Certificate and Diploma, both available at two levels, Ordinary and Higher. Both could be gained by full-time, part-time day, or evening study, or a combination of these modes. By September 1976 the TEC had approved 290 courses for starting in the academic year 1976–7. The BEC's first statement of policy, made in March

1976, promised Certificates and Diplomas at three levels: General, National, and Higher.

In December 1976 the Secretary of State, Mrs Shirley Williams, set up a Further Education Curriculum Review and Development Unit, described as being the counterpart to the Schools Council.

City and Guilds Certificates

Courses in a very large number of skilled trades are offered by the City and Guilds of London Institute (CGLI), which was founded by the Corporation and certain Livery Companies of the City of London in 1878, and incorporated by Royal Charter in 1900. Its Certificates have long had national – and indeed international – currency. For most trades there are two certificates: Intermediate and Final. The Intermediate Certificate ordinarily requires two years of attendance at College, with concurrent employment in the trade; the Final Certificate a further two years under the same conditions. For some trades the CGLI offers also a Full Technological Certificate; this requires at least another year's study. It is frequently regarded as a qualification for teaching the trade. The Institute also makes to distinguished craftsmen an Insignia award.

Courses leading to National and City and Guilds Certificates are largely taken by apprentices released for study by their employers for the equivalent of one working day a week. The number of 'day-release' students increased steadily until the late 1960s, but thereafter declined. By 1975 it had fallen to under 200,000, less than half the peak figure. There were always far more boys released than girls.

FE Colleges also prepare students for many other external examinations, including the GCE (required for exemption from the preliminary examinations of professional associations), CNAA degrees, examinations leading to membership of professional associations, and other nationally accredited qualifications.

Diploma in Art and Design

In 1961 a major reorganization was begun of the system of courses and examinations for students seeking professional qualifications in art. For over one hundred years the central Government had been responsible for these, but in 1958 the Minister of Education decided that the time had come for him to give up this responsibility. In 1959 he set up a National Advisory Council on Art Education to advise him on "all aspects of art education in establishments of further education".

At that time the Minister was making two awards: the Intermediate Certificate in Art and Crafts, and the National Diploma in Design (NDD). Candidates for the Intermediate Certificate had to be at least eighteen years old, and must have studied at an approved Art College or School for at least two years' full-time, or four years' part-time. As with National Certificates and Diplomas, the Colleges prepared their own syllabuses and set and marked their examinations, subject to the approval and assessment of the Ministry. Course work as well as examination results was taken into consideration in making awards. The conditions for the award of the NDD were similar. Candidates had to be at least nineteen. If they had already secured the Intermediate Certificate the Diploma course was two years' full-time; if not, three years. Candidates for the Diploma presented either a single subject, known as a Special subject, or two subjects, one being a main subject and the other an additional subject.

In 1960 the National Advisory Council on Art Education recommended that there should be broader diploma courses. Instead of specializing in particular subjects, students should work within one of four broad areas of study: fine art, graphic design, three-dimensional design, and textile/fashion.[17] The Minister accepted the recommendations, and announced that the last normal examinations for the Intermediate Certificate and the NDD would be held in 1963 and 1965 respectively. These awards would be replaced by a Diploma in Art and Design (DipAD), approximating in standard to a first degree. There would also be opportunities for post-diploma study (later, a higher diploma was created), and 'vocational' courses for students not intending to take DipAD courses. The first DipAD courses started in 1963, and the first graduates passed out in 1966. But there was much criticism, especially by students, of the DipAD courses and examinations; and in 1968, following demonstrative protests about this and other art college grievances, a joint committee of the National Advisory Council and the National Council for DipAD was set up. In 1970 this committee recommended the introduction of a four-year sandwich course biased towards industrial and professional practice in design.[18]

In 1974 the National Council for the Diploma in Art and Design was merged with the CNAA, and the DipAD replaced by a degree.

Agricultural Education

Up to 1959 the responsibility for agricultural education provided by LEAs was shared between the Minister of Agriculture, Fisheries and Food and the Minister of Education; but from 1 April 1959 full responsibility was transferred to the Minister of Education. This provision is of two kinds: part-time courses, day and/or evening, in FE Colleges, and full-time courses, ordinarily of one year's duration, in Farm Institutes,[19] of which in 1976 there were over forty maintained or assisted by LEAs. The courses are mainly residential, and it is ordinarily a condition of acceptance into one that the candidate shall have spent at least one year in employment or training on the land. On 1 April 1964 administrative responsibility for five agricultural colleges[20] was transferred from the Minister of Agriculture to the Secretary of State for Education and Science. These Colleges – four only since 1970, Studley having been closed – do more advanced work than the Institutes. They offer courses leading to their own

Diplomas, to OND and HND, and to post-Diploma awards. The National College of Agricultural Engineering, at Silsoe in Bedfordshire, prepares for CNAA degrees. Nine universities offer degrees in agriculture, and four in horticulture.

To advise their constituent LEAs there are in England nine Regional Advisory Councils for Further Education (RACs); in Wales the Welsh Joint Education Committee undertakes this function. These Councils are voluntary bodies established and financed by the LEAs in their regions. To co-ordinate their work, and to advise the Secretary of State upon national policy for vocational education there is a National Advisory Council on Education for Industry and Commerce (NACEIC), appointed by the Secretary of State.

From 1947 to 1961 the Minister of Education offered annually Technical State Scholarships, tenable at Universities, University Colleges and Colleges of Further Education. These were intended for young people, ordinarily under the age of twenty, in full-time employment. Under the Education Act 1962 the Minister's powers to award State Scholarships (except to students over the age of 25) were repealed, and a duty to make awards to all students who had been accepted for first degree or comparable courses was laid upon the LEAs. The Education Act 1975 extended this duty by requiring LEAs to make awards also to students on courses leading to the HND, the Diploma in Higher Education (Dip HE), or the Teacher's Certificate.

Adult Education

Non-vocational education for adults, in classes organized for formal instruction, is provided by:

1. Local Education Authorities.
2. 'Responsible Bodies', that is, bodies recognized for grant by the DES as being "responsible for the provision of liberal education for adults".
3. HM Forces.
4. Voluntary bodies, other than 'Responsible Bodies'.

1. LEAs provide non-vocational education for adults in Colleges of Further Education, in the residential Colleges and Centres of Adult Education which they maintain or assist, and in numerous short courses and conferences which they organize.

2. Among the 'Responsible Bodies' are twenty-three Universities in England and Wales. They exercise this function through a Department of Extra-Mural Studies, a Department of Adult Education, or, in a few cases, a School of Education. Working in close cooperation with the Universities, and organizing jointly with them numerous classes, is the Workers' Educational Association (WEA). Each of the districts of the WEA (there are 17 in England and Wales) is recognized by the Secretary of State as a 'Responsible Body'. Each (independently or jointly) offers single lectures, terminal courses (not fewer than ten

meetings), sessional courses (lasting one educational year, with not fewer than twenty meetings), three-year tutorial courses (which must be provided by a University), and other courses of various lengths, including vacation courses, the last usually residential, and sometimes conducted abroad. Most lectures and courses are open to the general public, but in recent years the WEA in particular has arranged, at the request of industrial and other organizations, courses solely for the members of such bodies. All lecture courses include time during each meeting for discussion of the lecture by members of the audience. The famous 'Three-year Tutorial Course', launched by the WEA in 1907, is now usually offered jointly by the University and the WEA; in this a select band of students studies intensively, at or near University standard, a subject of their choice through three consecutive winter sessions, meeting at least twenty-four times each session. Over recent years about 12,000 students have registered annually for tutorial courses.

The only other Responsible Body is the Welsh National Council of YMCAs. Every Responsible Body has to submit yearly the programme it proposes to provide, and an estimate of its cost, to the Secretary of State, who pays a direct grant towards the total teaching costs involved by the programme as he approves it. In determining the amount of grant he takes into consideration the standards of the courses proposed, the fees to be paid by the students, the needs of the area concerned, and the provision made by other bodies in that area.

3. The Department of Defence, which looks after the affairs of the Navy, Army, and Air Force, includes adult education in the educational services provided for members of HM forces. It works in cooperation with the Universities, the WEA and other voluntary bodies, and the LEAs, all of which admit members of the Forces to courses open to the general public, and if required arrange special courses for them. The Defence Department also maintains a scheme of correspondence courses for members of the Forces unable to attend organized courses in person; and while many of these correspondence courses are taken for vocational purposes, not all need be or are.

A Central Committee for Adult Education in HM Forces, representative of the Service Departments, the Universities, LEAs, and voluntary bodies, gives advice and provides an administrative centre for all Forces education.

4. Many other voluntary bodies provide opportunities for liberal adult education; they include learned societies, associations promoting appreciation of the arts, trade unions, youth organizations and the Churches.

In 1969 the Secretary of State appointed a committee, under the chairmanship of Sir Lionel Russell, formerly the CEO for Birmingham, "to assess the need for and review the provision of non-vocational adult education in England and Wales". The committee's report,[21] published in March 1973, recommended that the existing basic structure of provision should be retained. What was needed, said the committee, was a new spirit rather than new management.

A means of consultation and co-operation between all bodies engaged in adult education is provided by the National Institute of Adult Education (NIAE), which gives information and advice, conducts investigations, organizes confer-

An adult leisure class in sculpture

cnces, maintains a library, publishes a directory of adult education organizations, and establishes contacts with oversea bodies engaged in Adult Education.
The Institute is supported by membership fees, an annual grant from the DES,
and such profits as result from its publications. Most Universities and LEAs are
corporate members of the Institute.

In 1975, at the request of the Secretaries of State for Education and Science
and for Scotland the Institute established an Adult Literacy Resource Agency,
for which the Government made a grant of £1 million. Within a year over
55,000 adult illiterates were being taught to read and write (as compared with
under 10,000 previously) by the combined efforts of the BBC, the LEAs, and
voluntary bodies.

The Service of Youth

The provision of organized educational, social, and recreative facilities for
young people during their leisure hours was begun on a national scale by
voluntary effort in the second half of the nineteenth century, and up to the
outbreak of the Second World War continued to be made very largely by

voluntary organizations receiving little or no aid from public funds. But in November 1939 the British Government, remembering how through neglect youth had deteriorated during the First World War, decided that "the Board of Education shall undertake a direct responsibility for youth welfare", and proposed a "close association of local education authorities and voluntary bodies in full partnership in a common enterprise".[22] The Board set up a National Youth Committee, and urged all the LEAs for Higher Education[23] to set up local Youth Committees "to formulate an ordered policy" in their areas. The Youth Committees were not themselves to organize youth activities, but to advise their authorities how best they could help by (a) providing staff, office accommodation and clerical assistance, (b) making grants towards rent and upkeep of buildings, and provision and maintenance of equipment, and (c) providing instructors for physical recreation and crafts. All such aid would rank for 50 per cent grant from the Board of Education. This joint responsibility has been maintained, though the financial and administrative arrangements have been modified.

By the Education Act 1944 the Service of Youth became statutorily a part of FE, being covered by the requirement of Section 41(b) that it is the duty of the LEA to secure the provision of adequate facilities for "leisure-time occupation" in "organized cultural training and recreative activities. . . ."

During the following ten years or more progress was halting. In 1958 the Minister of Education appointed a departmental committee under the chairmanship of the Countess of Albemarle, and in February 1960 this committee presented a Report which expressed in incisive and pungent language the unease generally felt about the neglect of the Youth Service.[24] The Government accepted the committee's recommendations with almost startling alacrity; and set up a Youth Service Development Council, announced large building programmes for the next three years, and established a National College for the Training of Youth Leaders. These measures effected considerable improvement, but in the opinion of most workers in the Youth Service, not nearly enough.

During the 1960s most of the voluntary youth organizations re-examined their aims and functions, and as a result developed new programmes, many of which were broader than the previous ones, the needs and deeds of youth being seen in relation to society as a whole. Emphasis was laid upon this in a forward-looking report, *Youth and Community Work in the Seventies*, published by the Youth Service Development Council in 1969, and by a government social survey entitled *The Youth Service and similar provision for young people,* published in 1972.

The central direction of the Youth Service remains with the DES, and its local administration with the LEAs. The Youth Service Development Council advises the Secretary of State on the making of grants to voluntary bodies, especially for experiments and new developments. For these, and for local projects involving capital expenditure, grants are available under the Social and Physical Training Grant Regulations, 1939. The Secretary of State makes direct grants to recognized national voluntary youth organizations in aid of their headquarters administration. Since the Albemarle Report denominational youth organizations, previously excluded, have been added to the grant list. In 1976 the Secretary of State established a Youth Service Forum for England and Wales to advise national and local government, and all agencies making provision for youth service, upon national policy. Its membership includes representatives from the DES and other government departments, the LEA associations, and the staff associations of voluntary bodies.

The LEAs all have Youth, or Youth and Community, Committees, representative of the authority, of any minor local authorities within the area, of the voluntary youth organizations, the teachers, the religious denominations, the public health and careers services, and of the local civic and industrial life. Most authorities employ a full-time Youth, or Youth and Community, Officer, who in large or heavily populated areas will have one or more assistant officers. His business is to encourage the development of youth work generally throughout the area, supervise the work in any youth centres the authority may set up, maintain contact with the voluntary organizations, discussing with them and putting before his committee their applications for financial aid, secure instructors for classes in both maintained and voluntary clubs and centres, recruit youth leaders and arrange training courses for them.

The main bodies providing the Service of Youth can be grouped as follows:

(*a*) LEAs.
(*b*) Uniformed Voluntary Organizations.
(*c*) Non-uniformed 'club' organizations providing a general range of facilities.
(*d*) Non-uniformed organizations pursuing particular purposes or activities.

(*a*) Many LEAs run youth centres or – a recent trend – youth and community centres. Most of the youth centres are accommodated in schools, but a few are housed in purpose-built premises. The idea of youth and community centres has given rise to some interesting experiments; in 1972, for example, the ILEA opened in Islington a 'community complex' which included a Primary school, clubs for children, clubs for young people up to the age of twenty-one, and an adult education institute. Youth centres maintained by LEAs provide facilities for indoor games and hobbies, physical training, music, art, and drama, and for instruction in organized classes. The LEAs also aid the Youth Service in many other ways, ranging from training leaders to assisting unemployed, homeless, and disabled young people.

(*b*) The largest uniformed associations are:
The Scout Association.
The Girl Guides Association.
The Boys' Brigade.

Others include:
Army Cadet Force Association.

The Church Lads' Brigade.
The Girls' Brigade.
British Red Cross Society, Junior Section.
St. John Ambulance Brigade.
Sea Cadet Corps and Girls' Nautical Training Corps.

The Scouts' and Guides' Associations are so well known that it is unnecessary to describe here their aims and methods.

The Boys' Brigade, like the Scouts and Guides, has been widely copied overseas; it has branches in British Commonwealth countries, Denmark, Holland, and several 'developing' countries. Its main strength, however, is in the British Isles. One of the oldest uniformed organizations for boys, it was founded in 1883 by Mr W. A. (later Sir William) Smith, and has consistently pursued the aim laid down by the Founder:

> The advancement of Christ's Kingdom among Boys, and the promotion of habits of Obedience, Reverence, Discipline, Self-Respect, and all that tends towards a true Christian Manliness.

(*c*) Among the largest non-uniformed associations are:
The National Association of Youth Clubs (NAYC).
The National Association of Boys' Clubs (NABC).
YMCA Boys' Work Section.
YWCA.
Girls' Friendly Society.
Welsh Association of Youth Clubs.

(*d*) Associations pursuing particular purposes or activities include:
Community Service Volunteers.
Duke of Edinburgh's Award.
International Voluntary Service.
National Youth Theatre.
National Federation of Young Farmers' Clubs.
Co-operative Union Ltd (Education Department).
Welsh League of Youth (*Urdd Gobaith Cymru*).
Youth Hostels Assocation (YHA).

(*e*) Denominational organizations include:
Assocation for Jewish Youth.
Baptist Union (Young People's Department).
Church of England Youth Council.
Congregational Church in England and Wales (Youth and Children's Department).
Methodist Association of Youth Clubs.
Catholic Youth Service Council.
Presbyterian Church of England (Committee on Youth).
Provincial Youth Council of the Church in Wales.

All these and other associations are represented on the National Council for Voluntary Youth Services (formerly the Standing Conference of National Voluntary Youth Organizations), a body which exists to promote and sustain the interests of all, and in particular to present their views to the DES. There are also similarly representative regional Standing Conferences.

In June 1968 a State-sponsored youth organization, the Young Volunteer Force, was launched, with a Government grant of £100,000 spread over three years, its purpose being to get young people doing community service. The grant was later increased when the Force began to set up community development projects.

References

1 *Higher Education*, p. 2, para. 6.
2 At Rugby in Warwickshire.
3 The National College of Agricultural Engineering, College of Air Training, School of Automotive Studies, National Leathersellers College.
4 Mr H. A. Warren, in *Technical Education*, a booklet published by SCM Press, 1957, p. 5.
5 Battersea Polytechnic, London; Birmingham College of Technology; Bradford Institute of Technology; Brunel College of Technology, Acton; Cardiff College of Technology; Chelsea Polytechnic, London; Loughborough College of Technology; Merchant Venturers College, Bristol; Northampton Polytechnic, London; Royal Technical College, Salford.
6 Chelsea Polytechnic (London), and Cardiff College of Technology (Wales).
7 Sandwich courses had been used in England for a century, but this was the first time that they had been developed systematically on a national scale.
8 Report of the Committee appointed by the Prime Minister under the Chairmanship of Lord Robbins 1961-63. Cmnd. 2154, HMSO, 1963.
9 Cmnd. 3006, HMSO, 1966.
10 A Report by a Committee of Inquiry appointed by the Secretary of State for Education and Science, under the Chairmanship of Lord James of Rusholme. HMSO, 1972.
11 Cmnd. 5174, HMSO, 1972.
12 For further details see Chapter 11.
13 *Education in 1964*, being the Report of the Department of Education and Science. Cmnd. 2612, HMSO, 1965, p. 65.
14 Limited powers of conferring degrees had occasionally been granted to non-university institutions, e.g. St David's College, Lampeter.
15 Cmnd. 1254. See also Circular 1/61, issued simultaneously.
16 The chairman of the committee was Dr H. L. Haslegrave, who had recently retired from the Vice-Chancellorship of Loughborough University.
17 First Report of the National Advisory Council on Art Education ('Coldstream' Report). HMSO, 1960.
18 *The Structure of Art and Design Education in the Further Education Sector*. HMSO, 1970.
19 These establishments are variously called 'Institute', 'Centre', 'College', or 'School'. The most frequent title is 'College'.
20 Royal Agricultural College, Cirencester; Harper Adams Agricultural College, New-

port (Shropshire); Seale–Hayne Agricultural College, Newton Abbot; Shuttleworth Agricultural College, Biggleswade; Studley College, Studley (this, a residential college for women, was closed in 1970).
21 *Adult Education: A Plan for Development.* HMSO, 1973.
22 Board of Education Circular 1486, *The Service of Youth*, dated 27 November 1939.
23 The LEAs for Higher Education were the Councils of the County and County Boroughs.
24 *The Youth Service in England and Wales* ('Albemarle' Report). HMSO, 1960.

Further reading

BRISTOW, A., *Inside the Colleges of Further Education.* HMSO, 1970.

CANTOR, LEONARD M., and ROBERTS, I. FRANCIS, *Further Education in England and Wales.* Routledge & Kegan Paul, 2nd edition, 1972.

HARRISON, J. F. C., *Learning and Living 1790–1960.* Routledge & Kegan Paul, 1961.

HOGAN, J. M., *Impelled into Experiences* (story of the 'Outward Bound' movement). Educational Productions, 1969.

KELLY, THOMAS, *A History of Adult Education in Great Britain.* Liverpool University Press, 2nd edition, 1970.

LOWE, JOHN, *Adult Education in England and Wales.* Michael Joseph, 1970.

NIAE, *Year Book of Adult Education.*

PETERS, A. J., *British Further Education.* A critical textbook. Pergamon Press, 1967.

PRATT, JOHN, and BURGESS, TYRELL, *Polytechnics: A Report.* Pitman, 1974.

ROBINSON, E. E., *The New Polytechnics.* Cornmarket Press, and Penguin, 1968.

TEC and BEC. An 'Education' Digest on the Technician and Business Education Councils. Councils and Education Press, 1977.

VENABLES, P. F. R., *Technical Education.* Bell, 1955.

WARREN, H. A., *Technical Education (SCM 'Technics and Purpose' pamphlets).* SCM Press, 1957.

Official
Board of Education, 1900–39. Annual Reports.
Ministry of Education, 1947–63. Annual Reports.
Ministry of Education.
    Youth's Opportunity – Further Education in County Colleges (Pamphlet 3), 1950.
    Further Education (Pamphlet 8), 1947.
    Evening Institutes (Pamphlet 28), 1956.
    Technical Education (White Paper), Cmnd. 9703, 1956.
    The Youth Service in England and Wales. Cmnd. 929, 1960.
    Better Opportunities in Technical Education (White Paper), Cmnd. 1254, 1961.
    Forward from School. The links between School and Further Education, 1962.
    All from H.M. Stationery Office.
Department of Education and Science. *Full-time Agricultural Education in England and Wales.* (Published annually.)
Reports on Education.
    Education for Commerce (No. 15), October 1964.
    Advice and Advance (No. 19), February 1965.
    Grants and Awards (No. 24), September 1965.

The Technical Colleges (No. 2, revised), April 1966.

The Youth Service (No. 5, revised), September 1966.

Education for Management (No. 33), January 1967.

Industrial Training and Education (No. 35), April 1967.

A Going Concern (policy for the arts), September 1968.

The Polytechnics (No. 65), September 1970.

A Plan for Polytechnics and Other Colleges (White Paper), Cmnd. 3006, 1966.

National Advisory Council on Education for Industry and Commerce. *Report of the Committee on Technician Courses and Examinations* ('Haslegrave' Report), 1969.

Youth Service Development Council. *Youth and Community Service in the Seventies*, 1969.

National Council for Art Education. *The Structure of Art and Design Education in the Further Education Sector*, 1970.

Teacher Education and Training ('James' Report), 1972.

Government Social Survey. *The Youth Service and similar provision for young people*, 1972.

Education: A framework for Expansion (White Paper). Cmnd. 5174, 1972.

Adult Education: A Plan for Development ('Russell' Report), 1973.

All from HM Stationery Office.

| # University Education

In 1976 there were in England and Wales thirty-five Universities, including the 'Open University'.

Oxford	Twelfth century
Cambridge	Early thirteenth century
Durham	1832
London	1836
Victoria University of Manchester	1880[1]
Wales	1893
Birmingham	1900
Liverpool	1903
Leeds	1904
Sheffield	1905
Bristol	1909
Reading	1926
Nottingham	1948
Southampton	1952
Hull	1954
Exeter	1955
Leicester	1957
Sussex	1961
Keele	1962
Newcastle	1963
East Anglia	1963
York	1963
Essex	1964
Lancaster	1964
Kent at Canterbury	1965
Warwick	1965
Aston in Birmingham	1966
Bath University of Technology[2]	1966
Bradford	1966
Brunel	1966
City[3]	1966

Loughborough University of Technology 1966
Surrey[4]   1966
Salford   1967
The Open University   1969

Of the ten CATs, eight (Aston to Salford above) became full universities. Chelsea Polytechnic became, in 1966, a School of the University of London, and Cardiff College of Technology, in 1968, the Institute of Science and Technology of the University of Wales (UWIST).

In 1966 the Royal Charter of the Manchester College of Science and Technology was altered to enable the College to become the University of Manchester Institute of Science and Technology (UMIST).

The Universities of Oxford and Cambridge are combinations of autonomous collegiate societies acting together, under statutes, for purposes of university work. In 1976 there were thirty-four Colleges and Societies at Oxford and twenty-nine at Cambridge. Durham was until 1963 a federation of two 'Divisions', located respectively at Durham and Newcastle upon Tyne. Durham University is organized on a collegiate pattern (it was originally modelled on Oxford), with Halls of Residence having the status of Colleges of the University. London University is a federation of a great number of various institutions: in 1976 it comprised fifteen non-medical 'Schools of the University' (these included the two Colleges, University (1826) and King's (1829), which gave it birth), thirteen undergraduate and fifteen postgraduate medical and dental schools, thirteen University institutes for advanced studies, and twelve non-University institutions having teachers recognized by the the University for the purpose of preparing students for its internal degrees. The University of Wales is a federation of seven institutions, located at Aberystwyth in central Wales, Bangor in north Wales, Cardiff, Lampeter, and Swansea in south Wales. They include the Welsh National School of Medicine at Cardiff, which has the status of 'School of the University' and the University of Wales Institute of Science and Technology (UWIST). The other Universities have a unitary organization, though several have attached to them associated or affiliated colleges or other institutions, one or two of them overseas.

The University of Keele, which started in 1950 as the University College of North Staffordshire, and was granted full university status in 1962, has several features which differentiate it from the other universities. For most students (originally for all) the undergraduate course lasts four years. In the first year they take a course which covers Western civilization and the physical and social sciences. In the following three years they must study both humane and scientific subjects. Originally, the University College was wholly residential, for staff as well as students, and the University has remained very largely residential. Because of its unique pattern of studies Keele was as a University College empowered to grant its own Bachelor's degree – a privilege never before granted to a University College in the United Kingdom.

The modern English Universities from Birmingham to Keele attained full

University status only after a period (in some cases many years) as University Colleges, during which they built up their academic standards by preparing students for external degrees of London University. The new foundations of the 1960s (Sussex to Warwick) were made full Universities from the start. The CATs were not required to serve any apprenticeship as University Colleges; this would, indeed, have been superogatory, since all had been for years doing graduate and post-graduate work.

University Government

The Universities are independent and self-governing bodies. This despite the fact that three-quarters of their income comes from public funds, and up to 90 per cent of their expenditure on capital projects. At Oxford and Cambridge the government of the University (as distinct from that of the Colleges) is completely in the hands of members of the University. At Oxford the ultimate legislative body is 'Convocation', which comprises all holders of the MA and certain higher degrees whose names are on the University's books. But Convocation meets only rarely; its functions are restricted to authorizing the affixing of the University seal, conferring honorary degrees, and making a final decision about legislation carried by the vote of not less than two-thirds of the members present in the 'Congregation of the University'. Congregation, on which sit the teaching and senior administrative staff of the University, enacts but does not initiate legislation; its function is to decide about measures submitted to it by the 'Hebdomadal Council', a body of some twenty-three persons, including the Chancellor (the titular Head of the University), the Vice-Chancellor (the executive Head), and eighteen members elected by Congregation. It is in the Hebdomadal Council that most University policy is shaped and executive decisions are taken. General supervision of teaching (except College teaching) and examinations is maintained by the 'General Board of the Faculties', and the organization of these matters is done by the Boards of the various Faculties. Financial administration is the responsibility of the 'Curators of the University Chest'.

At Cambridge the supreme legislative body is the 'Regent House', which comprises the university officers, the heads of colleges, the members, secretaries and assistant secretaries of faculties, boards and syndicates, and the fellows of colleges. One of the functions of the Regent House is to elect the 'Council of the Senate', which is the corresponding body to the Oxford Hebdomadal Council, and like it the chief source of policy and executive action. The 'Senate', comprising all holders of the MA or a higher degree, elects the Chancellor and can hear appeals from decisions of the Regent House, but otherwise has only formal duties. As at Oxford, there are a 'General Board of the Faculties' and Faculty Boards; and there are also 'Syndicates' in charge of other University affairs. Financial administration is the responsibility of a 'Financial Board'.

At both Oxford and Cambridge the Colleges are self-governing corporate bodies regulated by their own statutes, and having their own property and income. They do not receive any grants from public funds. The government of a College is in the hands of a 'Master' (or an officer with a comparable title),[5] and a body of 'Fellows', whose number is fixed by the College statutes. The Colleges are not completely independent bodies: they cannot alter their statutes without the approval of both the University and the Queen in Council; they are bound by some University statutes, including those regulating elections to professorial Fellowships and the presentation and auditing of accounts; and most Fellows are also members of the University staff and so subject to its rules.

The governmental machinery at other Universities is in many respects strikingly different from that at Oxford or Cambridge, but the really fundamental difference is that persons not holding University appointments constitute an important and influential element in it. Many of these lay members are elected as representatives of outside bodies, including statutory bodies.

The structure of government in the modern Universities (except London and Wales) is everywhere on a similar pattern, though with differences in detail. The supreme governing body is the 'Court', a very large body which includes representatives of the local civic authorities, of the political, religious, social, educational, professional, industrial, and commercial life of its area, of the professorial and non-professorial staff of the University, and of other Universities. The Court meets ordinarily once a year only, to receive the annual report made to it by the Vice-Chancellor on the University's work and the financial accounts, and to appoint (or re-appoint) certain lay officers, such as the Pro-Chancellors (the Chancellor's deputies) and the Treasurer. The Court as a rule appoints the Chancellor, and in some Universities the Vice-Chancellor also. In the modern Universities the Vice-Chancellorship is a permanent appointment; this is another feature which distinguishes their government from that of Oxford, Cambridge, London and Wales, where the Vice-Chancellorship is held in rotation, for periods of from two to four years, by senior members of the academic staff.

The chief executive body is the 'Council', a much smaller but still sizeable body (its membership may exceed fifty) of lay and academic persons, the former mostly appointed either by the Court or by neighbouring local authorities or other bodies, the latter mostly by the University Senate. The Council administers the University's finances; it also actually makes the appointments to the academic staff (including, usually, that of Vice-Chancellor) though as a rule only by approving recommendations made by the Senate; and confirms (or on rare occasions rejects) changes in academic regulations submitted to it by the Senate. Though ultimate control of academic matters lies with the Council, the effective decisions in this field are made by the Senate. Cases have been known of disagreement between Senate and Council, but in general the confirmation by Council of recommendations by Senate is purely formal.

Membership of Senate has altered – in some cases considerably – in recent years. Up to the 1960s it consisted ordinarily of the professors and a few representatives of the non-professorial staff. As a result of demands for wider participation in policy-making, more non-professorial staff and, at most universities, some students, were made members. The Vice-Chancellor is *ex-officio* chairman. Senate receives reports and recommendations from the Faculty Boards – presented by their Deans, who are ordinarily senior professors serving in rotation for two or three years each – makes recommendations for appointments to the academic staff, and is responsible for the teaching and discipline of undergraduate students and for the approval of post-graduate studies and research projects.

At London a body called the 'Court' controls the University's finances, and has charge of all its property, funds, and investments. The supreme governing and executive body for all academic matters is the 'Senate'. The London University Senate is differently constituted from the Senates of the other modern Universities in that it contains lay members as well as members of the academic staff, and that its members are appointed, not members by right of status. It functions largely through six standing committees: the Academic Council, the Council for External Students, the Council for Extra-Mural Students, the University Entrance and School Examinations Council, the Joint Finance and General Purposes Committee, and the Joint Committee of the Court and the Senate for Collective Planning. Another unique feature of the government of London University is the large part played in it by 'Convocation', a body comprising all graduates of the University who have applied for membership and paid the required fee. Convocation elects the Chancellor, appoints nearly one-third (eighteen out of fifty-nine) of the members of Senate, and has the right to express to both Court and Senate its opinion about "any matter relating to the University" – a right it has not infrequently exercised with telling effect.

The University of Wales, like other modern Universities, has a very large Court, which is mainly an examining and degree granting body. A relatively small Council deals with finance, and an Academic Board with academic matters. Each College has a Council and a Senate.

For many years most British Universities have had staff-student committees handling matters of joint concern. In 1968, however, there arose a strong demand from students for participation in university government and policy making. After considerable discussion the Committee of Vice-Chancellors and Principals and the National Union of Students issued in October a joint statement covering a wide range of topics, including decision-making, the content of courses, teaching methods, examinations, discipline and freedom of speech. The statement identified three broad areas of operation for committees on which students might be represented or at which their views should be considered: (i) the entire field of student welfare, including health services, catering facilities, and provision of accommodation; (ii) curriculum and courses, teaching methods, major organizational matters, university planning and development; and (iii) appointment and promotion of members of staff, and admission of students. In (i) there should be varying degrees of student participation; in (ii) students' views should be taken into account, but "the ultimate decision must be that of the statutorily responsible body"; in (iii) "student presence would be inappropriate", but students' views on the general principles involved should be considered.

Despite the differences in the structure of government in the Universities, one characteristic is common to all, and it is of fundamental importance: business flows upwards, not downwards as is the case in many industrial and commercial organizations. Policy does not originate in Council or Senate, and least of all in the Court. Academic policy originates in a Department or a Faculty Board, and is discussed thoroughly in one or (usually) both of these places before being presented as a recommendation to Senate. Similarly, administrative and financial policy is thrashed out in a Standing Committee before being presented to Council. The rule is not absolute, especially in these days of rapid growth and development, but it is very nearly so, especially in respect of academic business. University writers have indeed claimed that their system of government is one of the most democratic in the world, in that everyone concerned has opportunity to have his say about matters which affect him.[6]

There is no body officially representative of the Universities as a whole. In recent years the Committee of Vice-Chancellors and Principals (CVCP), on which sit the Vice-Chancellors and Principals of all the Universities in Great Britain, has become increasingly recognized as their spokesman in consultations and negotiations between the British Universities and the British Government; but this Committee is not empowered to commit the Universities (or any single University) to accept any proposal or take any particular course of action. If the Committee feels that any act of policy is desirable, each Vice-Chancellor then has to attempt to persuade his University to feel the same.

The Association of University Teachers (AUT), which is representative of teachers of all ranks in the Universities of Great Britain, has the right to negotiate with the Government about all matters affecting the professional rights of University teachers. The National Union of Students (NUS) plays an active part in promoting and defending the interest of student members of Universities.

University Finance

Public expenditure on University education has risen astronomically since the 1939–45 war. Up to 1939 Parliamentary grants to Universities for capital expenditure were rare, and were always in aid of special projects. By 1970 the annual capital grant was between £25 and £30 million, and was covering almost all new building. Recurrent grant, which was slightly over £2 million a year in 1939, was well over £150 million. All this money was coming from the central Government. In addition, the LEAs, upon whom had been laid in 1962 the duty of grant-aiding all students offered University places, were expending over £100 million on this account, and were further making grants to individual Universities totalling several million pounds. During the 1970s the nation's precarious economic situation severely curbed expenditure, both capital and recurrent.

Until 1967 University expenditure was not subject to public audit. From 1 January 1968, in accordance with a recommendation of the Public Accounts Committee (PAC), it became a condition of grant to Universities that their books and records in respect of grant should be open to the inspection of the Government Comptroller and Auditor General.

University Grants Committee

Parliamentary grants to the British Universities are made through the agency of the University Grants Committee (UGC). This committee – the successor to several *ad hoc* committees – was first appointed in 1919, "to inquire into the financial needs of University education in the United Kingdom and to advise the Government as to the application of any grants that may be made by Parliament towards meeting them". Until 1943 it remained a small body, and its membership was restricted to persons not employed full-time by a University. In 1943 this restriction was abandoned, and the committee was enlarged to sixteen persons, exclusive of its secretaries, who are Civil Servants. In 1946 the committee's terms of reference were considerably broadened and made more explicit, and in 1952 they were further amended, to read:

> To inquire into the financial needs of University education in Great Britain; to advise the Government as to the application of any grants made by Parliament towards meeting them; to collect, examine, and make available information relating to University education throughout the United Kingdom; and to assist, in consultation with the Universities and other bodies concerned, the preparation and execution of such plans for the development of the Universities as may from time to time be required in order to ensure that they are fully adequate to national needs.

The final words of that charge, it will be seen, imply a measure of Governmental direction of University development. When these terms of reference were announced there were people who feared that they might lead to complete Governmental control of the Universities. While those extreme fears have not been realized, there is no doubt that the size and characteristics of University expansion since then have been very considerably determined by Governmental decisions – usually financial decisions.

In 1964 the Government decided to give University status to the CATs and some of Scotland's Central Institutions. This involved a larger responsibility for the UGC, whose membership was increased to twenty-two, and whose salaried staff (henceforth drawn mainly from DES) more than doubled, from 50 to 112, between 1964 and 1968. In 1976 the UGC had a full-time chairman and nineteen part-time members: fourteen from Universities, two each from schools and industry, and one from local administration.

Members of the UGC make periodical visits to all the institutions on its grant list[7] to discuss with their representatives the development plans and financial needs of their Universities or Colleges. The UGC holds periodical meetings with representatives of the Committee of Vice-Chancellors and Principals, and, if requested, meets representatives of the Association of University Teachers (AUT) and the National Union of Students (NUS). Much of its detailed work is done by sub-committees and advisory panels composed of members of the main committee and members appointed from outside for reason of their knowledge and experience in the fields concerned. *Ad hoc* committees and study groups are also appointed to examine specific questions of policy.

Parliamentary grants to the Universities for recurrent expenditure are agreed for five years at a time, though grants are paid annually. Every five years the Universities submit detailed estimates of their financial needs for the coming quinquennium to the UGC. After scrutiny of these estimates the UGC indicates to the Government, through the Secretary of State for Education and Science, the total amount which it recommends should be granted to the Universities during the quinquennium under survey.[8] The Government is concerned with the total grant only; how this shall be divided between the Universities is decided by the UGC in consultation with the individual Universities. A University is, in theory, under no obligation (except in the case of grants 'earmarked' for specific purposes) to spend its grant exactly as laid down in the estimates previously discussed with the UGC. In practice, no significant departure would be made unless this had been discussed with the UGC. Under the strain of inflation the quinquennial system was modified in the 1970s.

Academic Organization

For purposes of teaching, research, and examination, most of the Universities are divided into Faculties,[9] which are subdivided into subject departments. In the present century the number of Faculties has tended to increase considerably; in addition to the traditional Arts and Science (or Philosophy), Law, Theology, and Medicine, most Universities now have a Faculty of Engineering, and other Faculties such as, for example, Architecture, Economics, Industrial Relations, Town and County Planning, Education, Music. Of new departments there has been an immense proliferation, especially in the fields of pure and applied science, but including also such different subjects as Drama, Marketing, Operational Research, and Computer Studies.

The head of a Faculty is the Dean, elected for a period of years from among the professors. (Occasionally a full-time permanent Dean of the Medical Faculty is appointed.) Most departments are headed by Professors; the other ranks in the academic staff are Readers, Senior Lecturers and Lecturers. Attached to the academic staff are also Research Fellows and Research Assistants.

The principal administrative officers are the Vice-Chancellor, who is also the academic Head, and responsible for all aspects of University life, the Registrar (or Secretary), responsible for official business and records, and the Bursar, who administers the finances, and is responsible for the buildings and property of the University.

The University of Lancaster

There are two main bodies of full-time students: under-graduates and post-graduates; in English Universities the former are in a large majority (in 1976 approximately four to one). There are also a few hundreds following courses leading to non-graduate qualifications, most of which are called Diplomas.[10] All the Universities except Oxford and Cambridge have also part-time students; the number fluctuates, and has tended to increase in recent years; in 1975 it was over 20,000.

Admission

The Universities have absolute rights over the admission of students. Before inserting a student's name *in matricula* (i.e. on the register), every University demands evidence that he is intellectually able enough to undertake the course he proposes and has reached a sufficiently high standard of attainment to embark upon it. The capacity and attainments of applicants for courses leading to first degrees are judged by performance at either (*a*) an entrance examination conducted by the University concerned, or (*b*) an examination of equal or higher standard, success in which, provided stated conditions are satisfied, the University will accept in lieu of a pass in its own entrance examination.

In England and Wales the Universities have accepted success in any of the examinations conferring the General Certificate of Education (GCE) as exempting candidates from their own entrance examinations, subject to such conditions as they may from time to time lay down. In 1949 the Committee of Vice-Chancellors and Principals agreed to the following:

Applicants for entry to a University must:

(*a*)   Have obtained a pass in English Language and in either four or five other subjects; and

(*b*)   These subjects must include (i) a language other than English, and (ii) either mathematics or an approved science; and

(*c*)   At least two of the subjects must be passed at the Advanced Level; and

(*d*)   Candidates who offer only four subjects in addition to English Language must pass at one and the same sitting in two subjects at the Advanced Level and in one other subject not related to the subjects at the Advanced Level.

In 1966 the conditions were considerably simplified. Not more than five GCE subject passes would be required. Applicants must possess (or secure before entry) either (*a*) two A levels and three O levels, or (*b*) three A levels and one O level. About one-third of the Universities were prepared to accept also a third pattern: three A levels, one of which must be in General Studies. A few Universities required English to be among the subjects passed. Otherwise, no subjects were compulsory; and no limit was put on the number of times a candidate sat in order to get the required number of passes. A few Universities, including Oxford and Cambridge, did not accept these conditions.

Examinations comparable with the GCE (e.g. the Scottish Certificate of Education) are accepted, with similar conditions. *The foregoing are minimum academic qualifications.* Where (as often happens) there is pressure of applicants the bare minimum will be unlikely to secure admittance; and departments ordinarily require that particular subjects shall have been passed, and at a high level. Most Universities are, however, prepared to consider an applicant with unusual qualifications, especially if he/she is of mature age. Several Universities have experimented with the admission of applicants lacking the normal academic qualifications.

Applications for admission to first degree and first diploma courses in the Universities of England and Wales must be made through the Universities Central Council on Admissions (UCCA),[11] which was established in 1962, and was in full operation from 1965. Detailed instructions on how to apply are contained in the *Handbook* available from UCCA. Applications must be made between 1 September and 15 December (for Oxford and Cambridge 1 September–15 October) in the year preceding the one in which entry is desired. These conditions apply to applicants from oversea countries as well as those resident in the United Kingdom.

The qualifications required for entry into higher degree courses vary with the subject of study. English Universities recognize for this purpose all British degrees (and occasionally other qualifications) and some degrees awarded in other countries. The list of these is available at any British University.

Scholarships and Awards

Well over 90 per cent of full-time University students in England and Wales receive grants, from public or private funds, which provide wholly or in part for the payment of their tuition fees and other expenses. The great majority of the grants are made from public funds.

The main sources of financial assistance are:

1. Scholarships, exhibitions, and other awards made by Universities and Colleges of Universities from funds held in trust by them for this purpose. Some of these awards are 'open', that is, available for competition by all qualified candidates. Some are 'closed', that is, restricted to members of a particular school or geographical district. The value of these awards is ordinarily insufficient to meet all the holders' expenses of tuition and maintenance; to meet this situation, supplemental grants are made from public funds to holders of 'open' awards.

2. Grants made by LEAs. This is much the largest source of financial assistance to students. From 1962–63 the Minister of Education ceased to give State scholarships (except to mature students), and LEAs became legally responsible for making grants to all persons ordinarily resident in their areas admitted to first degree or comparable courses in the United Kingdom.[12] The Minister remained responsible for awards to students doing post-graduate (or comparable) courses, students undergoing training as teachers, and students doing first degree (or comparable) courses who "have attained such age" as is laid down in Regulations (i.e are 'mature' students).[13] Since 1966 post-graduate awards have been made by the Secretary of State for Education and Science, the Minister of Agriculture and Fisheries, the Research Councils and the LEAs. State scholarships to 'mature' students, that is, persons aged twenty-five and upwards, have always been limited to 30 a year, and awarded for honours degree courses in liberal rather than vocational studies.

The grants made by the Secretary of State and the LEAs are made under powers conferred respectively by Sections 100 and 81 of the Education Act 1944, as amended by the Education Act 1962.

University Life and Work

Before the 1939–45 war the younger universities – the 'civic' or 'provincial' universities, as they were called – drew their students largely from their immediate neighbourhoods. Since then all the universities have become 'national' Universities, that is, they draw their students from all over the country, – though in most of the civic Universities there will still be found a considerable minority whose homes are in the surrounding region.

The proportion of University students living at home fell steadily between 1945 and 1965. The transformation of the CATs into Universities briefly slowed this trend, but some of these new Universities soon began providing themselves with residential accommodation. The main forms of residence are colleges, halls of residence, and, a recent development, houses and flats, some with communal facilities, provided by the University, or by an association of students.

New building, and the adaptation of existing premises, had by 1976 made available University-provided residential accommodation for over 40 per cent of students. The proportion of students in lodgings, for long the largest, had fallen to under 40 per cent. and of students living at home to under 20 per cent. These were aggregate proportions; individual Universities varied greatly. Cambridge, Durham, Keele, and Loughborough had three-quarters or more of their students in residence, Aston, Bath, and Salford under one-quarter.

There are two fundamental differences between membership of an Oxford or Cambridge College, and membership of a Hall of Residence in a modern University. First, a student in College is a member of a Society; and he remains a member of that Collegiate Society not only throughout his University career but throughout his life. While he is at the University he has the right – and in some particulars the duty – to participate in the communal facilities of his College, even though he may be resident in lodgings, as he almost always will be during part of his University life. A student in a Hall of Residence is not a member of a Society having an independent existence. His stay in Hall may or may not cover the whole of his University career (usually it does not), but whenever he ceases to reside there he ceases ordinarily to be a member. Secondly, the Oxford and Cambridge Colleges have by their Statutes teaching and tutorial responsibilities for their students. Halls of Residence are not bound by such obligations, and, not being independent corporations, cannot undertake them, other than on an informal and voluntary basis, except by consent of the University.

It is a cardinal principle in British Universities that the main responsibility for the ordering of his life, and for progress in his studies, lies with the student. He is informed about the courses of lectures, the seminars, tutorials, laboratory classes, and so on which are available to him, and told at which, if any, of these his attendance is compulsory. In most cases it is not, but in all the effective decision at the time rests with him. True, a student who frequently fails to attend, especially at meetings specified as compulsory, and whose work is unsatisfactory, will be asked to explain why. If he persists in non-attendance, and his work continues to be less than satisfactory, he may be suspended. So, too, may the student who repeatedly fails to pass the required examinations. Statistics about failure rates in British Universities are infrequent and unreliable, but figures collected by the UGC and other bodies suggest that on average about 13 to 14 per cent of students leave without securing degrees. This average, however, conceals wide variations (from 3 to 30 per cent) in both Universities and subjects.

Degrees and Diplomas

The structure of degrees awarded by the Universities of England and Wales is in details quite complicated, but in outline simple. There are four grades: Bachelor,[14] Master, Doctor of Philosophy (PhD), and senior Doctor. Possession of a Bachelor's degree is still usually a prerequisite for proceeding to a higher degree, but exceptions to this rule are increasing. Two main types of course lead to a Bachelor's degree. Each is known by various names: Special or Honours, and General or Pass or Ordinary. The fundamental distinction is that in an Honours or Special course the student concentrates upon one field (or two closely related fields) of knowledge, in a General or Ordinary or Pass course he is required to study three or four subjects, but to a lower level.[15] Some Universities, especially among the newer ones, are experimenting with courses of combined or integrated studies. The minimum period of continuous full-time study for a Bachelor's degree is three years; this is the usual period, but for some Honours degrees four years are required. The technological Universities (ex-CATs) rely very largely upon sandwich courses; for such courses the minimum period is four years.

At Oxford a Bachelor can proceed to the degree of Master of Arts (MA), without further examination, after seven years from matriculating, and on payment of the statutory fee. At Cambridge the same rule obtains, but the period is six years from the end of the student's first term, provided at least two years have elapsed since his admission as Bachelor. Elsewhere the Master's degree can only be secured by following a prescribed or approved course of study for not less than one academic year and by satisfying the examiners in written examinations and/or presenting a thesis on an approved topic. The PhD degree can only be secured by presenting a thesis embodying the results of original research; like the Master's, this degree cannot be obtained within one academic year of securing the Bachelor's degee, and it normally takes three or four years' full-time study. Both the Master's and the PhD degrees can ordinarily be secured by either full-time or part-time study. Senior Doctorates – e.g. DLitt, DSc DD, LLD – are ordinarily awarded to distinguished scholars who have made significant contributions to knowledge in their particular fields of study.

London is unique among British Universities in having had for over a century a complete structure of 'external' degrees as well as a normal one of 'internal' degrees. These external degrees could until recently be secured by students living anywhere, without attendance at the University, by passing the required examinations at a centre approved by the University. This structure, which dates from 1858, came into being originally because of the impossibility, due to the conflicting statutes of its constituent members, of making London a teaching University, and of the consequent necessity (if there was to be a University of London) of restricting its function to that of an examining body. By one of the happiest ironies of history this arrangement, born of dire necessity, has been of the greatest value in assisting institutions of higher education throughout the British Commonwealth and Empire to achieve full University status. By following the London University degree courses and taking the London examinations they established academic standards which justified the granting of a University charter. All the University Colleges in England and Wales up to 1957, except North Staffordshire, and many of those in existing or former British Dominions, Colonies or Protectorates followed this route. From 1945 London made 'special' arrangements with aspiring University Colleges at home and oversea whereby the College shared with London the framing of its own syllabuses and the marking of its own degree examinations over a period of some years before applying for a University Charter.

In the 1970s London University began to limit the availability of its external degrees, excluding students in FE colleges in England and Wales.

Social and Recreative Activities

At all the Universities opportunities are available for participating in a very wide range of cultural, social, and recreative activities. A few of these opportunities will be for staff only, and perhaps rather more will be joint staff and student enterprises, but the great majority will be primarily for students only, and will be initiated and conducted by them. Except at Oxford and Cambridge, where much of this side of University life is centred in the Colleges, the headquarters of these activities is the Students' Union, a building owned by the University but administered by the students. The controlling body, the Students' Representative Council (SRC), is elected annually from among themselves by the students, and headed by a student President, who may be given a 'sabbatical year', with a salary (paid by the Union), to enable him/her to concentrate on presidential duties without detriment to academic studies. Ordinarily, all students become members of the Union automatically on entry into the University, and a fixed annual grant is made in respect of this throughout their stay. The proportion of students which makes habitual use of the Union by regular participation in the club and society activities which it sponsors, varies; it is said in some universities to be as low as one-third, but in most it is probably much larger. Not all university clubs and societies are sponsored by the Union; it is open to any group of students to band together for any lawful purpose, but in order to use Union facilities and to qualify for a grant from Union funds any student club or society must have its constitution approved by the SRC.

The Students' Union building contains a hall (or halls) for meetings, concerts, and stage plays; committee and games rooms; a bar (or bars) and a refectory, all managed by the SRC. All universities provide playing fields, sometimes extensive, most have a gymnasium, and some have swimming-baths. Since 1945 many universities have developed Student Health Services, staffed by full-time doctors and nurses, giving psychological as well as medical assistance. Students are normally required to register with the Student Health Service.

The Open University

The Open University, originally conceived of as 'The University of the Air', because it was expected to teach almost exclusively by television and radio, was granted a Royal Charter on 1 June 1969, and opened in January 1971 with some 25,000 students. The University's headquarters are at Milton Keynes in Buckinghamshire.

The purpose of the Open University is, in the words of the committee which planned it, "to provide opportunities, at both undergraduate and post-graduate level, of higher education to all those who, for any reason, have been or are being precluded from achieving their aims through an existing institution of higher education".[16] The University is thus concerned essentially with older students than those who make up the great majority in the other universities. During its first two years no one under the age of 21 was admitted, but in 1974 a small experiment was begun, a few hundred students aged between 18 and 21 being accepted for a two-year project designed to discover how suitable the University's teaching methods were for this age-group.

These methods comprise correspondence courses, television and radio broadcasts, local discussion groups, and short residential courses, including an annual summer school which is compulsory.

There are no formal academic requirements for entry, but all applicants are screened, and the point at which they start in a course is determined by their academic qualifications or experience. The University's degrees are obtained by securing 'Credits', each of which signifies success in a one-year subject syllabus. Ordinarily, a student may not take more than two of these in any one academic year. Six Credits are required for a BA pass degree, and eight for BA honours.[17] Entrants with good academic qualifications need not obtain so many; of the students who started in 1972, for example, 24 per cent were excused three Credits, 18 per cent two, and eight per cent one.

Like other modern English universities, the Open University is governed by a Council of academics and laymen which is the executive body, and a Senate, which is the academic authority. There are student as well as staff representatives on the Council. As both staff and students are widely dispersed, the University (which accepts students from the whole of the United Kingdom) has divided its territory into twelve Regions. For each of these there is a Regional Assembly, open to all full-time, part-time, and tutorial staff, and all registered students in the Region. A Regional Assembly elects staff and student representatives to the General Assembly, which also includes members appointed by the Senate. The General Assembly may express an opinion to Senate on any matter affecting the work and interests of the University.

The Open University is financed by (1) Government grant made through the DES, (2) students' fees (which may be subsidized by LEAs), and (3) the sale of its publications, at home and abroad. The TV and radio broadcasts are produced by the BBC, which is represented on both Council and Senate, while the University is represented on the BBC's Further Education Advisory Council, its broadcasts being processed in the BBC's FE Department.

References

1 As a federal University, which it remained until 1903. Then, the federation was dissolved, the constituent colleges of Leeds and Liverpool became Universities, and the Victoria University was given a new charter constituting it a unitary University.
2 Formerly the Bristol College of Science and Technology.
3 Formerly the Northampton College of Advanced Technology, in London, to which the title 'City' applies.
4 Formerly the Battersea College of Technology, London.
5 'Master' is the most frequent title, especially at Cambridge. But President, Principal, Provost, Rector, Warden, and Dean are also used, and at one women's college in Cambridge, Mistress.
6 See, for example, Sir Eric Ashby's *Technology and the Academics*. Macmillan, 1958.
7 The UGC grant list includes all the Universities and University Colleges in Great Britain, and a few other institutions which have been accorded University status, e.g. the London and Manchester Business Schools.
8 Supplementary grants to meet special circumstances may be (and not infrequently are) made within the quinquennium.
9 At Oxford and Cambridge, which are primarily organized in colleges, the Faculties more nearly approach the Departments of other Universities. Some of the Universities founded in the 1960s substitute 'Schools' of cognate subjects (e.g. European Studies, Biological Studies) in place of Faculties.
10 There are also students doing post-graduate Diploma courses, e.g. to qualify as teachers.
11 P.O. Box 28, Cheltenham, Gloucestershire GL50 1HY.
12 See the Education Act 1962, Section 1, and the *University and Other Awards Regulations 1962* (SI 1962, No. 1689).
13 See the Education Act 1962, Section 3.
14 One or two Bachelor's degrees, e.g. Bachelor of Science (BSc) at Oxford, and Bachelor of Laws (LlB) at Cambridge, are higher degrees.
15 In examinations for General degrees candidates may be awarded Honours.
16 *The Open University*. Report of the Open University Planning Committee, 1969, para. 18.
17 At the Open University the Bachelor of Arts (BA) is the only first degree. It is awarded in all the six Faculties in being in 1976 (Arts, Educational Studies, Social Sciences, Mathematics, Science, Technology). The higher degrees are Bachelor of Philosophy (BPhil), Master of Philosophy (MPhil), and Doctor of Philosophy (PhD).

Further reading

ARMYTAGE, W. H. G., *Civic Universities*. Benn, 1955.
ASHBY, SIR ERIC, *Technology and the Academics*. Macmillan, 1958.
BELOFF, MICHAEL, *The Plateglass Universities*. Secker & Warburg, 1968.

BERDAHL, ROBERT O., *British Universities and the State*. Cambridge University Press, 1959.

DENT, H. C., *Universities in Transition*. Cohen & West, 1961.

HALSEY, A. H. and TROW, MARTIN, *The British Academics*. Faber, 1971.

MOUNTFORD, SIR JAMES, *British Universities*. Oxford University Press, 1966.

MARRIS, PETER, *The Experience of Higher Education*. Routledge & Kegan Paul, 1964.

PERRY, WALTER, *Open University*: A personal account by the first Vice-Chancellor. The Open University Press, 1977.

ROSE, JASPER and ZIMAN, JOHN, *Camford Observed*. Gollancz, 1964.

SILVER, H. and TEAGUE, S. J., *The History of British Universities 1800–1969 excluding Oxford and Cambridge: A Bibliography*. Society for Research into Higher Education, 1970.

TUNSTALL, JEREMY (ed.), *The Open University Opens*. Routledge & Kegan Paul, 1974.

Official

Higher Education. Report of the Committee appointed by the Prime Minister under the chairmanship of Lord Robbins 1961–63 ('Robbins' Report) Cmnd. 2154. HM Stationery Office, 1963.

Association of Commonwealth Universities. *Commonwealth Universities Yearbook*. Published annually.

University Grants Committee. *Returns from Universities and University Colleges in receipt of Exchequer grant*. (Annual.)
  University Grants Committee Annual Survey (published separately from 1962 to 1967).
  University Development (Quinquennial; last published number covers 1967–72).

CHAPTER 11 | Training of Teachers

The responsibility for ensuring that there is a sufficient number of trained teachers to staff the statutory system of public education lies with the Secretary of State for Education and Science. Section 62 of the Education Act 1944 lays down that he shall:

> make such arrangements as he considers expedient for securing that there shall be available sufficient facilities for the training of teachers . . . and accordingly, he . . . may give to any local education authority such directions as he thinks necessary requiring them to establish, maintain, or assist any training college or other institution or to provide or assist the provision of any other facilities specified in the direction.

Responsibility for ensuring that the courses and examinations leading to the Teacher's Certificate and other professional qualifications were of the requisite quality was undertaken for thirty years after the Second World War by Universities.[1] As the result of recommendations made in 1944 in the report of the McNair Committee on the supply, recruitment, and training of teachers and youth leaders,[2] between 1947 and 1955 all the universities except one (Cambridge) accepted this responsibility; and some of the Universities created in the 1960s also took it on.

To carry it out there was formed under the leadership of each University an Area Training Organization (ATO), representative of all the bodies in the area concerned with the education and training of teachers: the University, the recognized training establishments, the LEAs, and the teachers – though in many areas these gained representation only after a stern struggle. The Vice-Chancellor of the University was *ex officio* chairman of the governing body of the ATO.

To perform the academic and administrative duties falling to an ATO each University established an Institute of Education.[3] This was an integral part of the University, which appointed and paid its staff, and provided and maintained its premises. During the early years several of the directors of Institutes had a somewhat indeterminate status, but in course of time all except those at Oxford and Cambridge were accorded the rank of Professor, and most were made full members of Senate.

The principal functions of an Institute of Education were:

(1) To make administrative arrangements for the co-ordination, and approval by the University, of the courses, syllabuses, and examinations in the constituent member establishments of the ATO.
(2) To arrange courses and conferences for serving teachers and other people engaged in educational work in the ATO area, including courses leading to named qualifications, which were validated by the University.
(3) To provide and maintain a specialist library.
(4) To promote educational research and development.

There were in 1975 twenty-two ATOs in England, and one in Wales. The ATOs' areas varied greatly in size, population, and the number of their constituent member establishments. London, though territorially by no means the largest area, had over thirty colleges and departments of education, while Exeter, Hull, and Reading each had three only. But Exeter, in particular, had a huge territory, including Jersey and the Scilly Isles as well as Cornwall, Devon, and Dorset.

There were in 1975 five types of teacher training establishment:

University Departments of Education (UDEs);
Colleges of Education (until 1964 called Training Colleges);
Colleges of Education (Technical);
Polytechnic Departments of Education;
Art Training Centres (ATCs).

By far the most numerous were the Colleges of Education, of which there were over 160. Their principal task was the education and training of non-graduates, to whom they gave, from 1960, a three-year course (previously, except in some specialist colleges, it was two-year) leading to the Teacher's Certificate. Well-qualified 'mature' (i.e. older) students might have the three-year course compressed into two years, or even exceptionally into one. From 1965 selected students were offered a fourth year, in order to acquire a newly-created degree, the Bachelor of Education (BEd). A few colleges had for many years provided also one-year courses for graduates; in the 1960s other colleges were invited by the DES to do this; and soon the number of graduate students in the colleges had more than doubled, from about 300 to about 800.

Most of the Colleges of Education were 'general' colleges, that is, they trained non-specialist teachers, most of them for work in Primary schools. In the 1950s and 1960s there were small numbers of colleges devoted exclusively to training specialist teachers of domestic subjects or physical education; but by 1975 almost all of these had taken on also the training of non-specialist teachers.

Colleges of Education (Technical), UDEs, and ATCs provided courses of professional training only, most of them lasting one academic year. The four Colleges of Education (Technical) trained teachers for service in Further Education. They did not ordinarily accept applicants under the age of twenty-five unless they were graduates, and they required vocational as well as academic qualifications. In addition to one-year pre-service courses they also offered courses, of various lengths, to serving teachers, who attended on a day-release or sandwich basis. ATCs accepted only persons with professional qualifications in art or handicraft, whom they trained to be specialist teachers. Several of the general colleges of education also offered specialist one-year courses to students professionally qualified in music, speech and drama, dance and movement, handicraft, home economics, or rural science. UDEs accepted graduates only, whom they trained as specialists, predominantly for Secondary schools.

UDEs were provided, maintained, and staffed by their Universities. Four ATCs were provided by Universities,[4] the others by Art Colleges (or, latterly, Polytechnics). LEAs provided about two-thirds of the Colleges of Education, voluntary bodies (most denominational) the other third. Of about 50 Voluntary colleges, half were in association with the Church of England.

Colleges provided by LEAs were financed from a 'pool' to which all the local authorities contributed in proportion to the number of Primary and Secondary school pupils in their areas. Their contributions attracted the normal rate of DES grant. Voluntary colleges were grant-aided by the Secretary of State in respect of both capital and recurrent expenditure. As with voluntary schools, the capital grant, which was originally not to exceed 50 per cent of the approved expenditure, was progressively increased; by 1975 it had reached 85 per cent. In aid of the colleges' recurrent expenditure the Secretary of State paid the tuition fees for all 'recognized' students, and their boarding fees (if any), less the 'student's contribution'.[5] In respect of students in UDEs, and in ATCs maintained by universities, the Secretary of State made grants towards both tuition and maintenance.

A New Era

Throughout the thirty years up to 1975 all kinds of teacher-training establishments were devoted – as they always had been – exclusively to one purpose: the training of teachers. The White Paper *Education: A Framework for Expansion,* issued in December 1972, put an end to that. Colleges of Education were no longer to be monotechnic. They were to admit students not necessarily committed to teaching as their career, and consequently to provide courses that could lead to training for other careers. And, with possible exceptions, they were no longer to be linked with Universities, but integrated into the public sector of higher education, where:

> some colleges either singly or jointly should develop . . . into major institutions of higher education concentrating on the arts and human sciences, with particular reference to their application in teaching and other professions. Others will be encouraged to combine forces with neighbouring polytechnics or other colleges of further education to fill a somewhat similar role.[6]

Such colleges, said the White Paper, "will not be easily distinguishable by function from a polytechnic or other further education college."[7]

But not all the colleges could look forward to such prestigious futures. Many, said the White Paper, were "comparatively small and inconveniently located for development into larger general purpose institutions".

> Some of these will continue to be needed exclusively for purposes of teacher education with increasing emphasis on in-service rather than initial training. Some may seek greater strength by reciprocal arrangements with the Open University . . . Others may find a place in the expansion of teachers' and professional centres . . . Some . . . will have to be converted to new purposes; some may need to close.[8]

Discussions and negotiations, between maintained colleges of education and their LEAs, between LEAs and the DES, and between voluntary colleges and both central and local authorities, began almost immediately. The voluntary colleges, whose co-operation was essential to the success of the reorganization, proved amenable and, despite many difficult and some controversial decisions, by the summer of 1976 the futures of nearly all the colleges of education and polytechnic education departments seemed to have been decided. By 1981, said the DES, there would be about 40 institutions doing both further education and teacher education, about 30 colleges engaged almost wholly in training teachers (an unexpectedly large number), and about 25 education departments in polytechnics. Of the former 163 colleges of education only four would have merged with Universities; but 18 would have closed.

But in January 1977 the Secretary of State, Mrs Shirley Williams, announced a further reduction in the number of places in training establishments required in the 1980s: to 45,000, of which 10,000 would be for induction and in-service training, and 5,000 for graduates. This meant that more Colleges of Education would have to close, and more be merged with other institutions, than had been anticipated; and Mrs Williams published a list of 22 proposed closures (in addition to the 18 previously determined), and seven mergers. No firm decision on any had been made when this book went to press.

In pursuance of the Government's policy that, "outside the Universities, teacher education and higher and further education should be assimilated into a common system",[9] the Secretary of State laid before Parliament in July 1975 new FE Regulations, which came into operation on 1 August.[10] These formally incorporated the colleges of education (except those merging with Universities) into the public sector of higher education. They revoked the *Training of Teachers Regulations 1967* (and all subsequent amendments thereto), and thus ended:

(a) Provision for the overall supervision of teacher training through Area Training Organizations, including advice to the Secretary of State on the approval of persons as teachers in schools;

(b) Provisions relating to the management of maintained and voluntary [teacher training] establishments, the finance of the latter and the control of courses;

(c) Provisions for grant to students [being trained as teachers].[11]

Pending the establishment of new regional bodies (about which negotiations were still in progress) to take over the functions of the ATOs, the Secretary of State did not for the time being intend "to lay down as a condition of recognition of courses any provisions as to their duration or the minimum academic qualifications or age of entry". All that establishments were asked to do was to "continue to ensure that persons who are unsuitable on grounds of character or health are not admitted to courses which include practical experience in schools".[12]

That left unclear what would be the future role of the various 'clearing houses' through which all applications for entry into teacher training had previously been channelled: the Central Register and Clearing House for Colleges of Education (except the four 'Technical'), the graduate Teacher Training Registry for UDEs, and the Clearing House for ATCs. Actually they did not ordinarily depart from the previous conditions of admission.

Courses

The one-year UDE course, which continues as previously, consists of instruction in the principles and practice of education, including one or more periods of teaching under supervision in school. Many UDEs send their students on teaching practice for the whole of the spring term; but whatever arrangement is made, the time spent in schools is the equivalent of not less than 60 days. The courses in ATCs and Colleges of Education (Technical) are basically similar.

Many innovations may be expected during the coming years in the three- and four-year courses for non-graduates leading to the Teacher's Certificate or a first degree. Before the reorganization of teacher education the three-year (Teacher's Certificate) course comprised general education and professional training, pursued concurrently. For general education a student studied throughout the three years one, or two (according to the ATO's regulations), 'Main' subjects, and, in some areas, subsidiary subjects, usually for one or two years. Many ATOs also insisted upon a course in English for all students not taking this as a Main subject. The professional training consisted of instruction in the principles and practice of education, and included several periods of teaching under supervision in schools; these would amount in all to something between twelve and eighteen weeks.

That pattern is possible only if all students are on entry into college expecting to make teaching their career. For uncommitted students courses must be provided which can serve as a foundation for specialized training in any one of many careers. The answer to this situation suggested by the James Committee was a two-year course leading to a Diploma in Higher Education (DipHE).[13] The Government agreed, providing that the following conditions were fulfilled:

1 DipHE courses "must offer a genuine and useful addition to those forms of higher education already available, not a cheap substitute for any of them", and "be no less demanding intellectually than the first two years of a course

at degree level". Consequently, "the normal minimum entry qualification should be the same as for degrees or comparable courses".

2 They should be "offered by institutions in each of the main sectors of higher education", and "both general and specialised courses should be made available".

3 The DipHE "must be made generally acceptable as a terminal qualification and in particular as a qualification needed for entry to appropriate forms of employment".

4 DipHE courses "should also be seen as providing a foundation for further study and be designed, where appropriate, in such a way as to earn credit towards other qualifications, including degrees . . ."

5 They "should be validated by existing degree-awarding bodies", i.e. Universities and the CNAA.

The Government added that it intended that "DipHE students should qualify for mandatory awards".[14]

The DipHE got off to a slow start in the autumn of 1974, when only two courses were begun. But both these contained original features. Much the more unconventional (it shocked many educationists) was the one in the School for Independent Studies at the North East London Polytechnic (NELP). Here the students, some 70 in number, were made largely responsible for devising their own programmes; to help them to do this the course began with a six-week 'Planning Period' in which to work out, with advice from the staff, their individual courses. In July 1976, of 52 students still on the course 43 received the DipHE, and six others received a conditional award. The course was validated by the CNAA.

At the Bulmershe College of Higher Education in Berkshire the DipHE course was arranged to run alongside the first two years of the college's BEd course, with the difference that whereas all BEd students had to include an education 'focus' in their course as well as a main study selected from the humane or environmental studies, this was not an obligation on DipHE students – though there was available to them one called "applied social and educational studies". This course was also validated by the CNAA.

In 1975 a further nine polytechnics and colleges of education started courses, and by 1976 it was expected that in the academic year 1976–7 up to 40 courses would be available.[15] (Actually, there were about 50.)

Qualifications

Only 'Qualified Teachers' may hold permanent posts in maintained schools. A Qualified Teacher is defined in the *Further Education Regulations 1975* as:

a person who has successfully completed a course for the degree of Bachelor of Education, or a Certificate in Education or comparable qualification, of a UK university or the CNAA which has been approved by the Secretary of

State as a course for the initial training of teachers, and who has been accepted by the Secretary of State as a qualified teacher.[16]

It is expected that within the next few years the Teacher's Certificate will be phased out, and that all students training to be teachers will do a three-year course leading to a pass BEd, or a four-year course leading to an honours BEd; or a three- or four-year course leading to some other first degree, followed by a year of professional training.

In the past many colleges of education offered full-time 'Supplementary Courses', usually of one year's duration, to serving teachers, who were from 1955 seconded on full salary for the purpose. These courses were particularly intended for teachers wishing to equip themselves as specialists. Some colleges also offered similar part-time courses extending over two years. Both types of course could earn a specialist Certificate or Diploma. There were also one-term full-time courses; for these teachers could be seconded on full salary, but they did not receive any named qualification. Presumably, all these various kinds of supplementary courses will be incorporated into whatever scheme of in-service training for teachers evolves in the future.

College Life and Work

Before the 1939–45 war, teacher training colleges in England and Wales were small, mainly residential, and usually single-sex establishments. Most (54 out of 83) were voluntary colleges. After the war the situation changed radically in all these respects. The number of colleges was doubled, from 83 to over 160, of which over 100 were LEA colleges. Before the war, three-quarters of the colleges had fewer than 150 students; by 1970 less than one-third had under 500, and one in eight had over 1,000. (These were the peak figures; early in the 1970s intakes began to be reduced, and consequently numbers to fall.) Before the war, 60 colleges were for women only, and there were only seven co-educational colleges; by 1970 over 120 colleges were co-educational. Before the war, nearly all the colleges were wholly (or almost wholly) residential; by 1970 only 44 per cent of students were resident, 16 non-residential 'day' colleges had been opened, mainly for 'mature' students, and nearly 30 had established 'annexes' or 'outposts', all non-residential, at some distance from the college.

Students in UDEs were, and are, eligible for residential places in their universities; so too are students in university ATCs and other institutions where residential accommodation is available.

Instruction in all types of institutions training teachers is by lecture (though much less so than formerly), seminar, tutorial group, supervised and self-directed practical activities, and observation and teaching practice in schools. Most colleges of education had by 1975 well-equipped art studios, craft workshops, libraries, resource centres, and science laboratories; many had gymnasia, and increasing numbers language laboratories and closed-circuit television. Many had playing fields of their own, some extensive. In the new era begun in 1975–76 'freestanding' (i.e. not merged) colleges will presumably have to rely upon the facilities they already possess, but colleges which have amalgamated with polytechnics or other major colleges of further education will share a considerably wider range of facilities, especially in the fields of pure and applied science. Similarly, they should be able to extend their range – already wide – of extra-curricular activities. As previously, all students are automatically members of the Students' Union, which is run by a Students' Representative Council (SRC), and is usually affiliated to the National Union of Students (NUS). Their annual subscriptions are paid by the LEAs for maintained colleges, by the DES for voluntary.

Staffing

The head of a UDE is, except at Oxford, a Professor of Education. Assistant staff are recruited mainly from Secondary schools, though other schools, FE colleges (including former colleges of education), universities and, occasionally, other occupations are represented. Most are university graduates.

It is not possible at this moment in time to be certain about future academic staff titles in establishments which are training teachers. In the former colleges of education the head was styled Principal, and this title is retained in some at least of the 'freestanding' colleges. Where two or more former colleges of education have joined together to form an Institute of Higher Education the head is ordinarily called the Director. The head of a Polytechnic has always been a Director; where colleges of education have amalgamated with polytechnics the college head has ordinarily become an assistant director of the polytechnic.

In the former colleges of education there were four grades of assistant staff: Lecturer, Senior Lecturer, Principal Lecturer, and Deputy Principal. There were nationally fixed proportions of the staff in each of the first three grades. The salary scales for all academic staff were negotiated by a committee, the Pelham[17] committee, which was exclusively concerned with colleges of education. In 1975 the Pelham committee was amalgamated with the Burnham FE committee (and the Farm Institutes' committee) to form a new Burnham Further Education Committee, and the grades of assistant academic staff in all types of FE college were assimilated: Lecturer I, Lecturer II, Senior Lecturer, Principal Lecturer.

In the former colleges of education the academic staff were recruited largely from Primary and Secondary schools, except for the four Colleges of Education (Technical), where industrial, commercial, or professional experience was required in addition to academic qualifications. For the training of teachers staff will doubtless continue to be recruited largely from the schools, but in colleges providing a diversity of courses recruitment is bound to be on a somewhat different basis from that of a monotechnic.

In-service Training

It is accepted that a teacher's training is never completed. Both the James Report and the 1972 White Paper outlined proposals for a comprehensive system of in-service training. Up to the summer of 1976 no such system had been started, or seemed likely to start until the country's economic prospects improved. But it should not be overlooked that for many years there have been, in addition to Supplementary courses, other not inconsiderable facilities for in-service training. Short courses for serving teachers are offered by the DES, the LEAs, Universities, teachers' professional associations, and other bodies. Longer full-time courses, usually of one year's duration, and part-time courses extending over two or three years, are available at Institutes and Schools of Education. During the 1960s and 1970s there was a rapid growth of Teachers' Centres, where teachers meet for discussion, study, research, short courses, and social activities.

Advice to the Secretary of State

In 1949 a National Advisory Council on the Training and Supply of Teachers (NACTST) was established to advise the Minister of Education on all matters concerning the recruitment, supply, and training of teachers. Between 1951 and 1965 this Council produced nine published Reports, some very valuable. But in 1965 it was allowed to lapse, and not until 1973 was it replaced, by an Advisory Committee on the Supply and Training of Teachers (ACSTT). In 1976 this committee was still being used to give advice to the Secretary of State about the supply and training of teachers in the reorganized public sector of higher education.

References

1 At the time when they undertook responsibility five of the Universities – Nottingham, Southampton, Hull, Exeter, and Leicester – were still University colleges. All had become Universities by 1957.
2 *Teachers and Youth Leaders*. Report of the Committee appointed by the President of the Board of Education to consider the Supply, Recruitment and Training of Teachers and Youth Leaders, HMSO, 1944. Chapter 4, Sections 163–82.
3 The Universities of Manchester and Wales, for different reasons, established Schools of Education. These had a rather greater range of functions than Institutes. The Institute of Education at Cambridge was formed and financed by the Minister of Education.
4 London, which had two, Newcastle, and Reading.
5 'Recognized' students are those recognized by the DES as eligible for grants from public funds. All such grants are (except for some post-graduates) subject to a means

test; the 'student's contribution' is the amount due from his/her parents, or the student if independent of the parents.

6 *Education: A Framework for Expansion*, p. 44, Section 152.

7 ibid, p. 46, Section 160.

8 ibid, p. 44, Section 153.

9 Circular 5/75, *The Reorganization of Higher Education in the non-University Sector*, and *The Further Education Regulations 1975*, dated 18 July 1975. Para 2.

10 *The Further Education Regulations 1975*. (SI 1975/1054). HMSO, 1975.

11 Circular 5/75, para 3.

12 ibid, para 9.

13 *Teacher Education and Training*, p. 41, para 4.4.

14 *Education: A Framework for Expansion*, pp. 32–33. Mandatory awards are those grants to students which LEAs are obliged by law to make.

15 DES. *All about the Dip HE*. Information Sheets for School Leavers (available free from DES, Room 1/27, Elizabeth House, York Road, London SE1 7PH). HMSO, April 1976.

16 *The Further Education Regulations 1975*, Regulation 4(4).

17 The 'Pelham' Committee was named after its first chairman, Sir Henry Pelham, formerly Permanent Secretary to the Board of Education. It was established in 1945.

Further reading

DENT, H. C., *The Training of Teachers in England and Wales, 1800–1975*. Hodder & Stoughton, 1977.

HEWETT, STANLEY (ed.), *The Training of Teachers: A Factual Survey*. University of London Press, 1971.

KEMBLE, BRUCE (ed.), *Fit to Teach: A Private Inquiry into the Training of Teachers, with Recommendations*. Hutchinson Educational, 1971.

NIBLETT, W. R., HUMPHREYS, D. W., and FAIRHURST, J. R., *The University Connection* (the history of the University Institutes of Education). NFER Publishing Company, 1975.

TAYLOR, WILLIAM, *Society and the Education of Teachers*. Faber, 1969.

WILLEY, F. T., and MADDISON, R. E., *An Enquiry into Teacher Training* (based on the evidence submitted to a Select Committee of the House of Commons 1969–70). University of London Press, 1971.

Official

Board of Education. *Teachers and Youth Leaders* ('McNair' Report), 1944.

Ministry of Education. Annual Reports 1947–63.

Department of Education and Science. Annual Reports 1964 –.

Reports on Education: No. 49, *Colleges of Education*, October 1968. No. 68, *Probationary Teachers,* January 1971, No. 79, *Teacher Turnover*, May 1974, No. 80, *Pupil and Teacher Numbers*, No. 82, *Teachers for the 1980s: Statistical Projections and Calculations,* March 1975, No. 84, *Helping New Teachers: The Induction Year*, March 1976. (These Reports are obtainable free from the DES.)

Report of the Study Group on the Government of Colleges of Education ('Weaver' Report), 1966.

Select Committee on Education and Science. Session 1969—70. Teacher Training.

Teacher Education and Training ('James' Report), 1972.

Education: A Framework for Expansion (White Paper Cmnd No. 5174)

(All the official matter published by HM Stationery Office.)

CHAPTER 12 | A Unique Partnership

Reference has been made earlier in this book to the spirit of partnership which exists between the centre and the localities, and between statutory and voluntary bodies, in the planning, provision, and maintenance of the public system of education. I feel it is only fitting to conclude this brief survey of that system by attempting to show that in all its parts it is sustained by this spirit. The partnership is often subject to strains and tensions, sometimes severe; but as yet has survived these. I hope it always will, because it is this all-pervading partnership which makes the system work. Were it to cease an entirely different – and I think much less happy – system would emerge.

The first, and probably the most important, example of partnership is that between the home and the school. This is almost entirely a growth of the present century, and it is not yet either so highly developed or so intimate as it could, or should, be. But very remarkable progress has been made, progress which, in fact, has amounted to a revolution in the relationships between parents and teachers.

In the early years of this century the gates to the yards of Public Elementary schools were very frequently locked once the children were inside; and a permanent notice was often to be seen which said: "No parents allowed beyond this point." There was reason for the notice; almost the only parents who wished to gain admission were those who came to cause trouble – not infrequently to offer personal violence to a teacher. That state of affairs has virtually disappeared; with rare exceptions, parents now are everywhere welcomed into the school, and when they come their almost invariable desire is to seek advice or to consult with the head or other teachers for the benefit of their children. School yard gates are still occasionally to be found locked, but this is to guard young children against traffic dangers, not to keep parents out.

Numerous schools now have organized Parent-Teacher Associations (PTAs), which hold frequent meetings, to hear speakers on educational topics, to exchange ideas, or simply to have a pleasant social evening together – with the opportunity for private and informal consultations between individual parents and teachers. PTAs are probably more common in Primary than in Secondary schools, but are nevertheless to be found in large numbers in the latter. Much less common is the Parents' Association, whose exclusive title must not be taken to imply hostility to the teachers, or any desire to exclude them from its activities. It may have come into being simply because the Head Teacher, for reasons which appear sound to him, has been reluctant to take the initiative in forming a PTA. The usual reasons for such reluctance are fear that some parents might wish to interfere with the internal organization of the school, that the PTA might become dominated by active members of a political party, or that the association would fail to attract just those parents who stand in most need of the help it could give: the indifferent and apathetic parents who are always a problem for any school.

Both Parent-Teacher and Parents' Associations are often directly helpful to a school by providing it with amenities that are outside the LEA's budget or cannot immediately be provided from public funds; from large and costly items such as a swimming bath down to simple and inexpensive gifts like a few saplings for the school garden. Associations of both kinds also often provide helpers at school functions: speech days, athletic meetings, concerts, plays, and open days.

'Open Days' are a relatively new, and extremely popular, feature of the English educational system. On an Open Day the school is 'At Home' to all parents and friends who care to visit it. Samples of the children's work in every branch of the school curriculum are on display – usually in lavish abundance – with teachers and children in every room to explain and demonstrate. Frequently programmes of physical education, dancing, music, and drama are staged by teachers and pupils, and some schools add also talks by teachers on their work, or by outside speakers on local or general educational progress.

Quite a few LEAs expand the idea of school Open Days by holding periodically 'Education Weeks' during which all the schools in their areas are similarly 'At Home'; such 'weeks' usually offer, in addition to school displays and demonstrations, public meetings addressed by speakers of local or national eminence. A growing number of authorities – but not yet a large enough one – is using also other means of explaining the schools to the parents; notably through pamphlets describing their aims and facilities, which are sent to parents whose children are about to enter Primary or Secondary school.

Parallel with the growth of co-operation between home and school, but preceding it in point of time, and probably its principal cause, there has taken place a transformation of the relationships between the child and his teacher. In 1900 it would have been true to say that, with rare exceptions, children hated school, and the relationship between teacher and pupil was that of driver and driven. Today it is equally true to say that the great majority of children thoroughly enjoy school, and that the relations between pupils and teachers are cordial and friendly. The unhappy incidence of violent and disruptive behaviour in some schools must not obscure the fact that in many this never happens. It is, perhaps, hardly necessary to add that the relationships between teachers, and particularly those between head and assistants, have shown a similar trend; teachers could not have evoked a spirit of partnership between themselves and their pupils had they not previously developed this among themselves.

Contributing to the work of Primary and Secondary schools is a great host of people giving, voluntarily, the most varied services. At the outset it is pertinent to remind readers that all members of boards of managers and governors of schools, and of the councils and committees of LEAs give up leisure time to the performance of public duties; and in innumerable cases a very great deal of leisure time. Admittedly, many of these people are – in part at least – moved to undertake such service by motives other than a purely disinterested desire to help on the progress of education, and thus to advance the public weal; but that said, it must be added that a vast amount of zealous and disinterested work is done every year by them: and the schools would be much the poorer without it.

The same is true of the considerable number of persons who each year serve on committees and councils established to advise the Secretary of State, LEAs, and teachers' and administrators' professional associations. None of the members of any of these committees or councils is ever paid for his services. Membership of one of the Secretary of State's standing advisory bodies, in particular, is necessarily most demanding in time, and frequently involves considerable travel.

Comparable with such people are those who serve on the governing boards and committees of such autonomous national bodies set up to render specific services to the educational system as the National Institute of Adult Education (NIAE), the National Committee for Audio–Visual Aids in Education (NCAVAE), the National Foundation for Educational Research (NFER), the Schools Council and the University Grants Committee. And alongside these one can perhaps most appropriately mention two bodies which have for many years given most valuable service to the educational system, the BBC and the IBA.

These lists are far from being exhaustive. The schools daily receive aid, in the forms both of regular and occasional services, from public libraries, art galleries and museums, and increasingly from private industrial and commercial organizations. A welcome sign of the times has been the emergence of nation-wide 'pressure-group' organizations, such as the Confederation for the Advancement of State Education (CASE), and the Advisory Centre for Education (ACE) which, as its name implies advises as well as advocates.

One cannot pass from consideration of services given to the Primary and Secondary schools without particular mention of the part played by the religious denominations, and especially the Church of England and the Roman Catholic Church. Between them these bodies still provide nearly one-third of the maintained schools, and they share in the management or government of all these schools. But this is only part of the service they render, which ranges from the maintenance of diocesan Boards of Education to the nurture of voluntary societies promoting the study of aspects of religious education. The partnership between the Church and the State can still be, at moments, an uneasy one, but its continued existence is today never doubted save by extremists; and it is fair to say that it is as cordial and cooperative in England and Wales as in any country in the world – and much more so than in most.

In the field of Further Education the range and variety of co-operation between statutory and voluntary bodies are so large as to render detailed mention impossible in small space. They can, however, be broadly categorized under three heads: co-operation between industry (meaning all forms of gainful employment) and the education authorities in the promotion and organization of vocational education; co-operation between voluntary bodies and the education authorities in the promotion and provision of non-vocational adult education; and co-operation between voluntary bodies and the education authorities in the promotion and provision of educational, social, and recreative activities for adults and adolescents, and especially for the latter.

Finally, there exists a great deal of co-operation between the statutory bodies specifically concerned with education and those concerned with other parts of the national life. This co-operation takes place both at the centre and in the localities; by way of illustration it may perhaps suffice to point out that in the execution of his duty the Secretary of State for Education and Science and his officials are in constant touch with their opposite numbers in most Government departments.

In the concluding chapter of his book *Education in England* Sir William (now Lord) Alexander wrote: "Here, then, is this national system involving, as we have stressed, continual co-operation at all levels." I would like to conclude on the same note, with the same emphasis. It is often said that the English educational system is unique. So is every other national system of education. Our uniqueness is probably most marked in its very real dependence upon partnership between statutory authority and voluntary body.

Index